I'd Give My Left Boob for That … Oh, Wait, I Already Did

I'd Give My Left Boob for That ... Oh, Wait, I Already Did

Kimberly Fairchild

iUniverse, Inc.
New York Bloomington

I'd Give My Left Boob for That … Oh, Wait, I Already Did

iUniverse books may be ordered through booksellers or by contacting:

iUniverse
1663 Liberty Drive
Bloomington, IN 47403
www.iuniverse.com
1-800-Authors (1-800-288-4677)

ISBN: 978-1-4401-4979-5 (pbk)
ISBN: 978-1-4401-4978-8 (dj)
ISBN: 978-1-4401-4980-1 (ebk)

Printed in the United States of America

iUniverse rev. date: 6/24/2009

Other than family, all names used in this book are fictional

This book is dedicated to those who have lost their lives to cancer and to those who continue the fight.

Contents

Preface

I was having lunch one day with two good friends of mine. We were taking a break from doing some running around and trying to get donations, teams, and possibly corporate sponsors for the volunteer work we did with the American Cancer Society and the Relay For Life. We were discussing things we would like to accomplish and how much money we would like to raise during the upcoming event. The figures ranged from $50,000 to $100,000. One of the women said, "To heck with $100,000. We're going to shoot for the moon and go for $150,000."

At that point I got a face full of coffee, compliments of one of my friends, because I said, "I'd give my left boob for that. Oh, wait, I already did." She said that if I ever write a book I should give it that title.

I've thought about that comment for many years but never took the initiative to get it started. I'm not sure what got me started now, but I'm ready to tell my story. What makes my story unique from so many others? Not much, except that each story is unique in its own right. Therefore, my story is unique.

It's unique in a sense that I'm not rich, so I couldn't afford to have the best doctors or go to the best hospitals. I'm not famous, so I didn't have people knocking on my door to purchase the rights to my story or volunteering to publish my book due to my name. As far as all that stuff goes, I'm a nobody. I'm your normal, average, American female who struggles with things in everyday life. I sometimes live paycheck to paycheck. I sometimes buy my clothes at used clothing stores. I don't have large investments or large sums of money in the bank. I'm raising a daughter by myself, and I had cancer.

I cried. I laughed. I got scared, but I never lost hope. I had to fight hard to win the war against this disease. I didn't do it with lots of money or a movie career. I did it with strength, faith, courage, and love. I did it like 99 percent of other Americans.

It doesn't matter how we do it as long as we do it. This is my story of how *I* did it.

Acknowledgments

Thank you, God, for bringing me through it!

Brittany, you'll always be my baby girl. Thank you for being you and for never failing to put a smile on my face or make me laugh. You are truly a gift from God, and I admire the strength and courage you have shown during my battle with cancer. I love you!

Thank you to Vickie; your love and support during my battle with cancer helped get me through it. You were there for me through it all and never let me go through it alone. You were my rock.

To Lori and Roger, thank you for your love, support, encouragement, and prayers. Lori, you are not only my sister, but one of my best friends. Roger, my brother, I admire you and your relationship with God.

To all my friends, thank you for constantly listening to me rant and rave about writing this book.

A special thank you to Michelle C. for encouraging me to pursue my dream of writing this book. Thank you for being you. You mean so much to me.

Thank you to Michele G. for the first-pass editing of this book.

Finally, I would like to thank cancer. Thank you, cancer, for the wonderful friends I've met during my battle with you. Thank you, cancer, for helping me to appreciate every second of every day. Thank you, cancer, for showing me that with God, all things are possible. Thank you, cancer, for showing me that life is truly worth living no matter how hard it gets. Thank you, cancer, for helping me to strengthen my faith. Thank you, cancer, for showing me I'm a strong person. But most important, I want to thank you, cancer, for giving me the courage to stand up and kick your ass!

Chapter 1

My Reason to Write

As a little girl, I dreamed about writing a book involving the beautiful girl with long, blonde hair who was imprisoned in the attic by her ... You know how this story goes. Girl is more beautiful than her evil, wicked stepmother and stepsisters. Girl gets locked in the attic and made to do hard work because her only fault is that she is more beautiful than her stepmother and stepsisters. A handsome man named Fernando hears her cry for help and rushes to the bell tower on his black stallion named Aragon to save her, but is stopped short by the large, green, fire-breathing dragon keeping watch outside her window. I could go on, but we all know how it ends ... happily ever after.

That was my childhood fantasy for writing a book. The fairy tale book never came to fruition because the Cinderella story had already been written. Damn. Then I thought about writing a crime or romance novel, but didn't know enough about either one to even attempt it. Even though the idea of writing a book about fairy tales or crime or romance died, my dream of writing a book never did. It just took me thirty-three years to find a good pencil, a good subject, and a good place to start.

My good pencil is a BIC mechanical #2 pencil with 0.7 mm lead. My good subject is about my life and cancer. And my good place to start is by saying this: cancer sucks!

I never thought my schoolgirl heroic love story fantasy would change to something like a drama or horror story. It's not a horror story either, although it is somewhat scary. It's a story about my life: my life before cancer, my life with cancer, and my life after cancer.

It's my thoughts, my tears, my fears, my family and friendships, and most important, my jokes and laughter. It's my way of finally getting a chance to put my feelings down on paper and help relieve some stress about the possibility of a future battle with cancer.

I mention that possibility because I think about it often. If you've ever been diagnosed with cancer or you are battling it right now, you know what I'm talking about. If you're newly diagnosed, I'll be honest with you and tell you it's something you might think about all the time. It doesn't consume you and you should never let it, but you'll always think about it and often wonder when the other shoe will drop. Every new ache and pain might cause you to wonder. You might be on pins and needles each time you have to have a scan, an X-ray, or blood test. Furthermore, depending on the severity and makeup of your original cancer, your statistics for recurrence could be higher than others, which might make you more worried about its recurrence. This is the point I'm at in my life.

So, by writing this book, I'm focusing on three things. First, I want to show that while cancer is a serious disease and should be treated as such, you don't have to be so serious all the time when dealing with it. I try to relate how humor helped me through one of the most difficult and darkest times of my life.

Second, I want to show how cancer affects everyone around you, not just you. It affects your family and friends, your coworkers, your bosses, and even your pets. Those around you will take cues from you on how to act or what to say. If you're upbeat, they will be also. If you're sad and depressed about your situation, they will be too.

Third, if I can help just one person with my story and what I've been through, then everything I went through was 100 percent worth it. Deep in my heart, I believe that I had cancer to help someone. Maybe that person has already come and gone. Maybe that person has not yet been diagnosed with cancer. Maybe that person has a friend or family member who has been diagnosed with cancer. Maybe that person is you.

I apologize upfront if I offend anyone by what I've written in this book. I tend to look at things differently from most people, and I say exactly what I feel and think. I write in the same manner. Don't get me wrong: I took my cancer seriously, but not how I dealt with it or lived with it. People criticized me for that, as you'll read; thus the reason for my apology upfront.

I don't use words that make you smell the vibrant color of a tangerine crayon, see the angelic song of a morning dove, or taste the bitterness of the cold. I write in as simple terms as I possibly can because I don't own a dictionary and wouldn't know how to spell most of those words anyway.

This book is not filled with lots of medical jargon, pathology reports, or cancer statistics. I'm not a doctor and I don't play one on TV, so I won't pretend I know medically what I'm talking about. I still don't completely understand most of it myself.

As you read, feel free to laugh out loud, or cry, or nod your head in agreement. This book is to help you get more comfortable with your own cancer diagnosis if you find yourself in this situation. It's to help you understand what your friends and family who have been diagnosed might be thinking or feeling but are afraid to say. More important, it's a way to let cancer patients and their friends and family know that it's okay to laugh during some of the darkest times of their lives.

Chapter 2

Who I Am

Before I get deep into the story of my cancer battle, it is important to give you a little information about me, where I came from, how I grew up, and how that shaped who I am today. Learning about my childhood and my family life will help you understand a little more about who I am and why I did the things I did.

I was born in 1966 in Montgomery, West Virginia. The youngest of four children, I lived in a holler, a small valley between the mountains. Living there could give one a slight feeling of claustrophobia, because you have to look straight up to see blue sky. There was only one way in and one way out.

The house where I lived was nestled between a creek and a small, two-lane road. I could stand on the edge of my parents' front porch, lean out, and touch the sides of the coal trucks as they went past the house. This holler was very depressed, with some sections nicer than others. There were sections where houses were falling apart at the seams, and houses with junk cars in the front yards. There was even one house with a bathtub and a toilet in the front yard used as flower planters.

There were no gas stations, only one small, mom-and-pop grocery store, lots of churches, a few post offices and schools, and a few too many beer joints. There were larger grocery stores and Family Dollar stores about fifteen minutes away, but the closest place to go shopping at a mall or department store was more than forty-five minutes away.

We rode a bus to school, but if it didn't run, we had to walk to school with no shoes, in snow, uphill, both ways. Seriously, we did take the bus, but our towns were so small there were only a handful of kids on the bus. If we missed the bus we had to stay home because my mom didn't drive and my dad was already at work. Can you guess how many times we tried to pull this one off?

I lived with my parents, older brother, and two older sisters. I was very close to my mom and my sister Lori. She and I are only twenty-one months apart. Most people thought we were twins. My brother, Roger, who is thirteen years older than I, is the oldest. Then there's Vickie, who is ten years older than I. I hardly knew Vickie because she left home and joined the Air Force when I was only eight.

Lori and I were best friends growing up. There wasn't much to do living in a holler, so we spent most of our time outside either playing badminton, throwing the Frisbee, or passing a football. We had bikes we could ride, but our parents were kind of strict, so it wasn't too much fun because we couldn't go anywhere that was out of direct sight of our house. At night we'd catch lightening bugs or just sit on our porch and watch them light up the hillside behind our house. One of my favorite memories was when we went blackberry picking with our mom. We headed out with our buckets and did not return home until they were almost full. As soon as we would get home, Mom would let us eat a handful with a cold glass of milk, and then we would wait patiently while she baked a blackberry cobbler.

Growing up in the house with very religious and strict parents was rough. Dad had a wall-to-wall entertainment center that was full of music equipment. He had a receiver, a turntable, a reel-to-reel, a double cassette player, and even an eight-track player. I guess you could say it was a hobby of his, but one of his favorite pastimes was to make tapes for people from church of religious groups or church revivals that had been recorded. Lori and I were strictly forbidden to touch or play with dad's music equipment. Well, we learned very quickly how to operate the equipment. Dad shouldn't have asked us to help him make the tapes if he didn't want us to know how to use the equipment.

We loved music, country and southern rock, but couldn't play it unless Mom and Dad were gone. As the saying goes, "When the cat's away, the mice will play," and boy did we play. There was one song we particularly loved and we played it so loud that the neighbor across the street could hear it. Of course, we didn't learn that until years later when we were at Mom's funeral. He said he always knew when both mom and dad were gone because minutes after he would see the car pull out of the driveway, he'd hear us singing at the top of our lungs. Where was *American Idol* back then?

My interest in the military developed after Vickie left home and joined the Air Force. I remember getting letters from her describing the places she was stationed or had visited, and it made me jealous. I had never seen other places in the world and barely knew other places existed because we rarely traveled. If we left the confines of our holler, it was either to go shopping or to visit my grandmother's house, about two hours away. Imagine my surprise in school when I found out that Powellton, West Virginia, was not the center of the universe, and not only were there other states, there were other countries.

We did go on vacation, but it was always to the same places: the state fair of West Virginia or Gatlinburg, Tennessee. We always stayed at the same hotel when we went to Tennessee and did the same things because as Dad always said, "It was fun before, so I'm sure it'll be fun again." Yeah, right. It was fun when I was nine. I wanted to see other places. I never saw the ocean, for instance, until I was twenty-nine.

I needed to get outside the holler because there was nothing there. My parents couldn't afford to send me to college, and I didn't want to spend the rest of my life working in a small grocery store or flipping burgers at the local burger stand.

Before I graduated from high school in 1984, I enlisted in the Air Force. I was so excited that I was moving out of the holler and going to see the real world. On the other hand, I was scared and sad because I was moving out of the holler, where I knew everyone and everyone knew me. I was leaving my home. This home had been my protection and shelter for eighteen years. This home is where I knew love and felt love all my life. I was sad because I was leaving my two best friends: my mom and Lori.

So on a winter day, January 22, 1985, I boarded a plane for the first time in my life. When I say a plane, I mean a metal tube with wings, about five seats, wheels, and little propellers about the size of lawn mower blades. Yes, the proverbial puddle jumper. Remember in the beginning of the book when I said that I might offer up some advice? Well, let me start now. Don't ever let your first airplane ride be on a puddle jumper.

I hugged and kissed my mom and cried as if I'd never see her again. As we were standing in the middle of a parking lot in the frigid air, Mom hugged me close to her and said, "Remember when you feel you have no friends and nowhere to turn, you can always turn to God." How those words have stayed with me and helped me out in many a troubled time.

After tearful good-byes and hugs, my plane took off from a small airport in Beckley, West Virginia, and landed in Ohio, where I boarded a larger plane headed for San Antonio, Texas. There I would spend the next six weeks in basic training.

I felt like royalty when I stepped onto that larger plane. They served me food, I got to watch a movie, and they even gave me a pillow and a blanket. I had hit the jackpot. *So this is what they call first class,* I thought. Boy, was I a naïve country hick with a great deal to learn.

Basic training was tough, and I missed my mom more than anything. I got to talk to her on the phone a few times, and it was so good to hear her voice. I also took comfort in the letters she wrote me and the ones I wrote her. When Mom passed away six years later and we were cleaning out her stuff, I found a box full of all the cards and letters I had written to her when I was in basic training. I still have those letters tucked away in a safe place. I took them out and read them when I was battling cancer. They comforted me and made me feel like Mom was right there with me.

I worked hard in basic training and learned a lot about what I could and could not do. I learned about discipline and respect. I learned about military history and how to respect my country and flag. I learned about teamwork and physical fitness. But the most important thing I learned in basic training was that I hated folding my underwear in six-inch squares.

Six weeks of training were finally done. I graduated and headed to Denver, Colorado, where I would spend the next ten years of my life. Fortunately, my sister Vickie was stationed there as well. Remember, she left home when I was only eight, and I was now nineteen. She owned a home in Denver, so I moved in with her. Living together made it fun and easy getting to know each other. There were parties and clubs and funny recordings on our answering machine. We would go trick-or-treating for shots of alcohol on Halloween. She taught me how to drive a stick shift. She was my maid of honor at my wedding, she was there when my daughter, Brittany, was born, and she helped me through my divorce. We would often sit on her porch at midnight drinking peach schnapps and eating M&Ms, after which I would go lay down in the street and play dead bug.

Dead bug, you ask? Yes, dead bug. It's where you flop down on the ground on your back with your hands and feet in the air and shake and kick until you're "dead." If I wasn't playing dead bug, I was trying to sell myself as a K-Mart blue light special. Those were good times and when we became stationed together in Germany, it allowed us to have more.

Being in Germany was a thrill of a lifetime. The lush, green country hillsides and winding roads were what made Germany beautiful. This, in addition to the castles and historical locations, made it a wonderful place to be stationed. The food was outstanding, and for the most part, the weather was good. We quickly came to appreciate life in a foreign country. Brittany was settling into school (she started first grade in Germany), and I was settling into work and life.

We decided to live on base because I knew it would be a more secure environment for us. The apartment we lived in wasn't bad. It was a fourth-floor apartment with two bedrooms and nearly a thousand square feet. The bad thing about the fourth floor was there were no elevators, so grocery day was a bear. The good thing was we didn't have people walking past our door all hours of the day, and we couldn't hear the kids on the playground.

Base housing wasn't the greatest, but we made the best of it. Most of the housing buildings held twenty-four families. Being this far away from our family, we made strong bonds with our neighbors. In our building lived several people with whom we became good friends. Here we met the wonderful couple who became Brittany's godparents. At the corner of our building, we had a nice area with a picnic table where we would often have a potluck barbecue. We'd eat, laugh, and play games for hours.

We were at a large base and had many things to do. There was a base exchange (mini department store), a commissary (grocery store), two theaters, a bowling alley, and many other activities for families. Outside the base were plenty of places to eat and shop and even a nice pool that many of the Americans would often visit.

We had great times in Germany, but mine and Brittany's favorite was July 4 and the Christmas season. Around July 4, the base hosted the Freedom Fest, a four-day event for Americans to celebrate Independence Day. There were booths set up along the base parade grounds that sold food and drinks. The booths were normally staffed by military units to make money for their booster clubs. They sold everything from hotdogs and hamburgers to schwank steaks and drinks. However, the best part was the carnival with rides and games that lined the fairway.

The Freedom Fest included a huge flea market and bake sale. A tent was set up for bands to play until midnight. Every year they'd put on the biggest fireworks display I had seen. Patriotic music was blasted over the speaker system during the fireworks display, which made them more beautiful and meaningful.

I am a very patriotic person, and the Fourth of July is my favorite holiday. When I hear the national anthem, I get chills, and it brings tears to my eyes. If I'm at an event where they play the national anthem, I'm one of the first people to stand up and place my hand over my heart to show the utmost respect to our flag.

Another favorite pastime of ours while in Germany was during Christmas. Just about every small town in Germany had a Christmas market where we could buy crafts and food. The local favorite during that time of year was glühwein, a spiced hot wine. We could walk down any street during one of the Christmas markets and find hot chocolate, glühwein, and fresh roasted chestnuts.

Germany was also known for its great places to eat. One of our favorites was The Marathon. We could get schnitzel, a thin slice of veal coated in bread crumbs and fried, but The Marathon was known for their house specialty: pizza with a fried egg on top. It didn't sound too appetizing at first, but once I tasted it, I loved it. Another great place to get schnitzel was The Schnitzel Haus, which served a piece of schnitzel that took up the entire size of the plate. Everything else was served on the side. But our favorite place was The Cantina, a Mexican restaurant right outside the base. Most nights had about a thirty-minute wait for a table, as it was the favorite of many Americans. How funny is that, a Mexican restaurant in Germany?

The good part about being in the military and being stationed in Germany was traveling at the government's expense. In the military, we did things we refer to as a TDY, a temporary duty. This is where you go to another location to perform your job, go to school, or attend a meeting, seminar, or conference.

I was very fortunate to get to do a TDY in Rome and Naples, Italy, England, Belgium, Austria, France, and Greece. These places were absolutely beautiful, and if it hadn't been for being in the military, I probably never would have been able to visit them. Visiting Europe is one of those things you put on your list of things to do before you die.

Speaking of dying, that isn't something you probably think about all the time. It usually starts when something tragic happens to you or someone you love, but it doesn't consume your daily thoughts. I certainly didn't think about dying that often, but I eventually ended up there.

Chapter 3

How Did I End Up Here?

My health has never been the greatest due to family genes. My mother died of a massive heart attack when I was only twenty-five. She was only fifty-five. She also suffered from Type II diabetes for almost ten years before her death. My father died when I was thirty-five from several health issues, such as Alzheimer's and prostate cancer, so on the cancer front I thought I was safe because the last time I checked, I didn't have a prostate. I was sure I was invincible, at least to cancer. I figured I would have high blood pressure, check; diabetes, check; high cholesterol, check, and probably heart disease. Thank God I can't check that one off yet. So, all the while I was getting my heart, blood pressure, cholesterol, and sugar checked, cancer had snuck inside my body and took up residence inside my left breast.

I had no idea that I was on a path that would end up with my body and mind being bombed with the statement, "You have cancer." However, something happened on November 21, 2001, that would put me on an emotional roller-coaster ride leading me directly into those words—a ride that would also have me fighting for my life.

That day started out as an ordinary day. I got out of bed, took a shower, ate breakfast, kissed Brittany before I left for work, and left the house. Around 9:30 AM, I left the office to head to my doctor's appointment. I didn't want to go because it was one of "those" appointments, a get naked, hop on the table, put your feet in the stirrups, scoot down to the end of the table, and spread 'em cause you ain't got anything I haven't seen before appointments. This doctor hadn't seen "this" before because she was new. My family doctor was on vacation, so another doctor was brought in to take his place. Given the outcome, I guess this was God's way of watching out for me.

Up until the breast exam, things were going very smooth. The doctor and I were making idle chat while I was staring at the posters on the ceiling. Now, if you're a guy reading this you might ask yourself, "Posters on the ceiling?" Yes, what else are you supposed to look at while you're flat on your back with your legs spread wide, down at the end of the table, and your doctor has his hand in your … you get the idea.

After that fun-filled exam, she did the breast exam. We were still making idle chat when she stopped talking and had a concerned look on her face. Why do people do this? Just like when you're driving and looking for a building or street, you turn off or turn down the radio. Does the quiet help things you're trying to find come into view? As if they hear it's quiet and just give up by saying, "Damn, I'm here. You found me. I guess I can't hide anymore now that it's quiet." The doctor was concentrating on the left breast but remained quiet while she finished her exam. She would feel the left in a particular area and then move over to the right to feel in the same area.

She made a comment that I had very fibrocystic breasts and asked if I had ever been told that before. I had, in fact, been told that ever since I'd been having breast exams. I was also told if I stopped drinking caffeine it would help my fibrocystic condition. Caffeine aggravated the cysts and made them swell, thus increasing pain in the breasts. I was at that time a Pepsi-holic. Therefore, taking away my caffeine was like taking gas out of my car and trying to get it to go. It just wasn't going to happen.

After a few minutes, she stopped and looked at me with a very serious expression on her face. It was a look somewhere between serious and sympathetic. She then asked, "How long have you had this mass in your left breast?"

"Mass?" I asked. She went on to say that the reason she kept feeling both breasts was because cysts sometimes mimic themselves, and when there's one on one side, there will normally be an identical one on the other. The mass she was feeling on my left, unfortunately, didn't have a twin on the right.

She asked if I had ever had this checked out, and I told her I had seen my doctor in January. She asked what was done about it then. Nothing, I told her. She was a little surprised and asked me to explain. I told her that I had made an appointment in January 2001 because I was having pain in my left breast. When I got in to see the doctor, he asked me a few questions. Keep in mind that this doctor had been my family doctor for five years and had been doing my breast exams for that long as well, so he was very familiar with my breasts and the lumpiness of them.

> *I wasn't worried because I was too young to have cancer, I had no family history, and I was invincible.*

Instead of doing an exam, he asked "Are you currently on your period?"

"Yes."

"Did you quit drinking caffeine?"

"No."

"Do you have a family history of breast cancer?"

"No."

Those three questions and my one-word answers was all he needed to make my diagnosis, which was, "You're fine."

When I finished telling her the story, the doctor had a surprised look on her face. She couldn't believe he didn't offer to do a mammogram or an ultrasound. She asked me if it was still painful, and I said yes, it was at times.

The doctor asked me to get dressed and meet her in her office. When I walked in her office, she still had that same look on her face, and I knew something was up. I sat down, and she told me she was so sure the mass in my breast was more than just a cyst that she was sending me to the military hospital for a biopsy. The hospital was only fifteen minutes away from the base and was where we had to go for special medical appointments that couldn't be taken care of at the local family clinic.

No ultrasound? No mammogram? Straight to biopsy? I was

thinking, *What makes her so right in her conviction that I have to go this route?*

The doctor must have read my mind, because she said, "I've worked in breast health clinics for twenty-three years, and I know what I'm talking about."

Gulp.

At this point I became a little worried, but then again, I was only thirty-five, I had no family history, and breast cancer was a disease for old women, or so I thought. I stopped worrying because I was too young to have cancer and I was invincible. I wasn't going to let it affect me because I had a job to get back to.

The doctor took my information and said someone would set up my appointment for the biopsy. She also said it could take up to a week to get it scheduled but that someone from the General Surgery Clinic would call me and let me know the date and time of the biopsy. I thanked her and went back to my job and my normal life.

Three days passed, and I hadn't heard anything about my appointment. During the week, a few people asked me if I had gotten my biopsy appointment yet, and I said no. I figured that maybe the doctor believed I didn't need one after all, and that it would be a waste of time.

Day four came like any normal day. The phone rang; it was the General Surgery Clinic informing me that the biopsy was scheduled for Monday, December 3 at 9:30 AM.

Chapter 4

The Biopsy

I had no idea what to expect and was terrified of what it meant to have a biopsy. Since my sister Vickie and I were stationed together, I asked her to go with me. I wasn't sure of the procedure and how much pain I'd be in, so I asked her to drive. We went to the appointment, chatting about work and life as we drove. She said I looked nervous, and I gave her the "does a bear shit in the woods" look. Vickie reminded me about the biopsy she had done on her breast about a year before (which turned out to be just a cyst) and that it didn't hurt much. I trusted her, so I began to calm down a little.

When we arrived in the clinic, I was checked in and given a stack of papers to fill out that made my enlistment paperwork look small. We were finally called back into an exam room, where I was asked to remove everything from the waist up. Shortly after changing, the surgeon, Dr. Crawford, knocked on the door and came in. After a few brief introductions he asked me, "So what brings you in to the General Surgery Clinic today?"

Why do doctors do this? They know why I'm coming to see them. It's as if I made everything up, and he was giving me a chance to come clean and confess. Besides, I had just finished explaining it to his med-tech. Did he not write anything down? Did he need some remedial training on how to take notes when the patient was talking? It was just easier to explain it again, so I did. Then the fun began.

As most breast exams go, I was kneaded and poked and rubbed. After the exam he said he felt something, but he wanted to do an ultrasound to see what we were dealing with. He left the room and after a few minutes returned with a portable ultrasound machine. He probed around the lump and took a few measurements of the thing he kept referring to as a "cyst." After the ultrasound, he said he would like to do a fine-needle biopsy to be sure it was just a cyst.

Dr. Crawford left again and returned with a tray of instruments that made my eyes water. Vickie smiled and reminded me that it didn't hurt that much. The needle used to numb me wasn't too bad; it felt like a bee sting. Then came the biopsy needle. *Oh, boy, this is going to hurt,* was my first thought. The needle was extremely long but very thin. Vickie was right; it didn't hurt. After a few minutes of poking around with the needle, Dr. Crawford had a perplexed look on his face. He said he couldn't get any fluid from the cyst, so he wanted to do a core biopsy.

I wasn't sure what a core biopsy was, but he left the room and returned with a different tray of instruments and more lidocaine, the numbing agent. After a couple more numbing shots, he uncovered the tray with the other set of needles. At this moment my sister turned around and came over to the table where I was lying. She had an "oh, shit" look on her face. I asked her what was wrong, and she said, "I'm sorry I said it wasn't going to hurt."

After I saw the look on her face and got one look at the needle, I immediately understood. I'm sure the look on my face must have shown the same fear, because she looked at me and said, "It shouldn't be that painful because he's going to give you a few extra shots of lidocaine." If you say so.

As if Dr. Crawford wanted to torture me before he started to cause me physical pain, he piped up and said, "Yes, I'll give her a little extra lidocaine, but it only numbs the surface. She'll still feel the pinch of the biopsy." Didn't they teach these guys bedside manners in medical school? Now I was really scared, and my nerves started to get the best of me. I asked him if we could just stop talking and get it over with.

He stuck the needle into my left breast, and to my surprise it didn't hurt. *This is going to be quick and painless,* I thought. The further the needle went in, however, the more it hurt. I grabbed my sister's hand. It wasn't until he snipped a sample of tissue that I almost came off the table. The pain was bad, but the sound that accompanied the pain only intensified it. He removed the sample and placed in into a specimen cup. Finally, it was over. *That's it. I'm outta here.*

Not yet. Apparently, the first sample wasn't good enough, so Dr. Crawford wanted one more tissue sample. He reached once again for the needle to dose me up on lidocaine. I asked him not to give me the extra shot because I didn't want to get stuck just to get stuck again. "Just do the biopsy," I said. So he did. At that point I began to wonder if I had made the wrong decision in turning down the additional lidocaine.

Once again I grabbed for my sister's hand while enduring the probing needle, which would cut a small chunk of tissue from my left breast. Again the doctor pulled the needle from my breast and placed the second tissue sample into a different specimen cup and sealed the lids. I figured it was the proverbial sealing of my fate. My future was floating in a jar marked "Specimen." My future was dependent on what those two pieces of tissue showed when they were stained and dyed and placed under a microscope.

While the doctor was cleaning the incision site, I was able to get a good look at the specimens. Surely that wasn't what he took out of my body. He must have done something to it. I know healthy tissue is pink. The tissue samples floating in those jars were gray and slimy.

What did that mean? Maybe that's why he had the "I'm sorry" look on his face when he took out the first sample. Maybe that's why he had to take another sample. Dr. Crawford wasn't talking to me anymore. Why? What was going on? Things were happening in slow motion, and they were all fuzzy inside my head.

> *My future was dependent on those tissue samples floating inside the specimen jars.*

I suddenly became aware that my sister was asking me if I was doing okay. I looked down at my left breast. A Band-Aid covered the spot where the needle had invaded my body. The swelling and bruising had already started to manifest themselves, and I was sure the pain that accompanies them would come later. I was given instructions for keeping the area clean and was told to relax the next couple of days. Dr. Crawford handed me an appointment reminder to come back in on Friday to get my results.

Before I left, the doctor and I spoke about the results and what could be done about it if it were just a cyst. My options were to leave it alone or remove it completely. His recommendation was to just leave it alone. I told him I would rather have it removed because I would always wonder if it was growing or changing. I didn't want the constant worry, so I was very adamant about the lump being removed. He said we would discuss it on Friday when I came back to get the results. We shook hands and I left.

The ride home was quiet but kind of funny. Many of the roads in Germany are narrow, winding, made of cobblestone, and a little bumpy. There were several ways to get to and from the hospital, but the one well traveled was through a small village.

This route also gave us a few road choices depending on which security gate we were going to use to get onto the base. One road went through a quaint little shopping town and then turned sharply to the right. The road then went up a steep hill and through the woods, past an old but beautiful Catholic church and an orphanage. This was the most beautiful route due to the woods, especially in the fall, but it was also the most treacherous because it was straight uphill on very curvy roads.

The other route was safer, and it sent us through a neighborhood filled with lots of people who were always out walking. We chose this route, which made the drive from the hospital somewhat funny. The small streets meant our car was directly beside the sidewalks, so it was easy for people to see into our car as we drove past. Since this community was just outside a military base, there was nothing unusual about seeing two American women in uniform driving through the streets. However, seeing two American women in uniform driving through the streets with the passenger holding her boobs was a different story.

We got lots of looks and stares, but my left breast was killing me, and every tiny bump on the little cobblestone street only made it worse. We were certainly a sight to see, and we laughed all the way back to work. Little did we know that our laughter would eventually turn to tears.

After my biopsy, I returned to work and didn't discuss it much. I didn't need to because I knew nothing was wrong, and besides, I was invincible. I had a job to do and couldn't dwell on what may or may not happen. Everybody who asked me about my biopsy got the same answers: "It hurt" and "I get my results on Friday."

I didn't give much thought to what my results could mean, until one day when I was talking to my downstairs neighbor. She was a hair stylist who cut my hair and Brittany's hair. On Wednesday evening we went downstairs to get our hair cut.

After the haircut, we were sitting around talking, and she asked me if my biopsy site still hurt. I told her that it was a little sore, but it was more bruised than anything. I was telling her how I saw the samples, and they were gray, green, and slimy. She immediately got quiet and said, "Kim, that's not good."

That was the first time I thought about what the outcome could mean. I quickly put it out of my mind and started joking about the subject. I made a comment about losing my hair if I had cancer and had to go through chemotherapy. I told her if I lost my hair, I'd have to wear a wig; so on my way home, I would just drop off my wig for her to style and pick it up in the morning on my way to work. If I only knew how true that would be.

The week dragged on, and it seemed that others were more concerned about my biopsy results than I was. I knew people cared and were concerned about my well-being, but I felt if I didn't talk about it, then it wasn't real and the results wouldn't be bad. I would not have cancer.

Chapter 5

My Private Pearl Harbor

Friday, December 7, 2001. Pearl Harbor Day. It started out like any other day. I got up, showered, had breakfast, and got ready for work. The day was going to be busy. I had my appointment to get my biopsy results. I had lots to do at work because I had reports I always had to get done on Friday. My daughter had a dance that evening, and I was to attend a retirement ceremony for the husband of my good friend and exercise partner, Shelly.

Shelly was about five feet, five inches tall, with short, wavy brown hair. Her eyes lit up when she talked and her laughter was contagious. She had a calming tone when she talked, which was what I needed in a friend because she kept me calm. Shelly and I used to get up at 4:30 every morning and go for a walk. We lived in the same building, so we would meet outside, stretch, and go for our walk. It didn't matter what the weather was like; we always would walk Monday through Friday. We had a certain route we would take, approximately four miles long. The walks were great because it gave us a chance to get to know each other. We had become good friends, so there was no way I was going to miss this important event for her and her husband.

Shelly and I didn't walk that morning because she had a great deal to do and didn't want to get up early to walk. Before I left for work, I talked with Brittany and told her I would be home around 6:00 PM.

Her dance started at 7:00, so I wanted to be home before she left. We finished breakfast and I went to work. My appointment wasn't until 9:30 that morning, so I figured I would go to work and get started on my reports before having to leave again.

While I was at work, Vickie called and asked if I wanted her to go with me. I said, "No."

"What if it's bad news?" she asked.

"I want to hear it by myself."

"Well, then, what if it's good news?" she asked.

I said I wanted to hear that by myself too. She made a comment about my being stubborn and asked me to call her as soon as I got the results. I said I would and watched the clock for the next thirty minutes.

At 8:45 I headed out the door to go to my appointment. On the drive to the hospital, I passed a military bus bearing the Red Cross emblem. I knew where the bus was headed. It was headed to the hospital because it held wounded soldiers from the war in Afghanistan.

Not sure which route the bus would take, I decided to take a faster route and hit the autobahn, where I could put the pedal to the metal. I wanted to beat the bus to the hospital. I was sure it was going to the emergency room, where the soldiers would be seen by general surgeons. I know this sounds bad, but my appointment was with General Surgery, and I didn't want to get held up because I knew the soldiers would have priority.

I beat the bus to the hospital. Unfortunately, I had to drive around the parking lot a few times to find a place to park, because like most major hospitals, there were several entrances and several adjoining parking lots. The emergency room entrance was closest to where I needed to go to in the hospital, but there were hardly any parking places in that area. I drove around to the side of the hospital, where I found a place to park. I quickly made my way back around the corner to the emergency room entrance.

Damn. The bus was parked in front of the emergency room, and soldiers were starting to make their way off the bus. I walked in at the same time as a few of the other soldiers and was halfway down the hallway to the General Surgery Clinic when I heard a page over the hospital intercom system: "All general surgeons to the emergency room

STAT." Another damn. This meant I'd be waiting a long time, because my doctor was the head general surgeon.

I continued on to the clinic, albeit at a somewhat slower pace now, and checked in. I was asked to have a seat in the waiting area and told someone would be right with me. Yeah, right.

I took a seat, pulled out my bottle of water and a book, got comfortable, and settled in. I had just started reading my second page when the med-tech called my name. I repacked my belongings and headed for the exam room, where he took my vitals and asked me what I was there for. *Here we go again.* I wanted to mess with him and tell him I was there for my annual prostate exam, but I also wanted to get out of there in a timely manner, so I didn't want to confuse him. I told him I was there to get my biopsy results.

He asked another question that could have been answered if he had read my chart. "When did you have the biopsy done?" I almost punched him.

After the small chatter and redundant questions, he left me alone in the exam room to settle in once again with my book and water. At least they could have let me wait in the waiting room with a TV and other people. But no, I was stuck in an old room, painted battleship gray, with only a desk, an exam table, and two chairs.

I finally gave up looking for something to do and decided to return to reading my book. I had to reread the two pages I had read earlier because they didn't sink in. I thought I could finish the book, or at least a few chapters, before my doctor came back from the emergency room. However, that didn't happen. I barely made it to the end of rereading the first page when the door opened and in walked Dr. Crawford.

Without hesitation I looked at him and said, "You're here to tell me I have cancer, aren't you?" I thought he was going to pass out, or at least puke, while standing there. He said, "What makes you say that?"

"Well, when I came into the hospital, they paged all general surgeons to the emergency room STAT. You're the head general surgeon, and you're here with me. I'm not a dummy. Besides, the look on your face right now and when you did the biopsy kind of gives it away. So, am I right, or am I right?"

He was speechless. After a brief pause, he finally said, "Yes, I need to be here with you." He walked closer to me, and I could tell he wasn't messing around. Instead of sitting at his desk, he pulled up a chair close to mine. He sat down and put his hand on my arm and said, "You've got cancer."

I couldn't believe what I was hearing. His words slid so delicately out of his mouth but hit my eardrums and exploded into loud words, thoughts, and feelings in my head, deafening everything except for the sound of my own heartbeat. It was beating faster and faster, and I felt as if it were going to explode right at that moment. Then it hit me. I was having my own private Pearl Harbor Day.

With all these thoughts running through my head, I didn't hear a word Dr. Crawford was saying. He was sitting beside me, writing notes and drawing pictures. When he realized I wasn't listening, he asked me what the last word I had heard was.

"The 'you've got cancer' part," I said.

Little did I know he had just spent the last ten minutes telling me about options and surgeries. Little did *he* know I had just lived my entire life—past, present, and future—in that same ten minutes.

Chapter 6

The Fallout

I felt as if I had been in the doctor's office for an eternity, but it had been only about twenty minutes. He could tell I had lost focus and decided to ask what I was thinking and feeling. I told him I was trying to figure out how to tell my little girl, who was only twelve, her mom has cancer. He looked at me and said to be honest with her. *That's easy for you to say, Doc,* I thought. How do I tell my little girl this devastating news?

My daughter was the love of my life. She was the little miracle I was told I could never have. Ever since I was a little girl, I had told my mom that I wanted to have a baby girl when I grew up. When I turned twenty, I met a guy, fell in love, and got married a few months after turning twenty-one. We had a good marriage and had fun together. I wanted to have a baby right away, but I had trouble getting pregnant. I went to see several specialists, but they couldn't figure out what was wrong. I even went so far as to take fertility drugs for three months, but still nothing. So, with heavy hearts we decided to give up. We traded in our family car, bought a sports car, and then it happened. I got pregnant, but I wouldn't know it for another seven months.

Yes, it's true. I was seven months' pregnant before I found out. How is that possible? I have no idea. I had numerous pregnancy tests, both blood and urine, but every test came back negative. I wasn't showing, I hadn't gained weight, and I had no morning sickness. Eventually, I started having pains in my side, so the OB/GYN doctor decided to do an ultrasound. We were all surprised at what appeared before us on the screen. However, none was more surprised than I.

At first I thought I was dying because I wasn't sure what I was seeing. I had this thing inside my womb moving and flopping around like a fish out of water. I kept looking from the screen to my belly, back to the screen to make sure the picture was coming from me. My doctor, who was doing the ultrasound, almost passed out. She had been my doctor for many years and was even the one who gave me the fertility drugs. We were shocked when she measured the baby and determined I was almost seven months pregnant.

It was a quick pregnancy; I hardly had time to prepare. Exactly one week after my twenty-third birthday at 11:47 PM, I gave birth to a six-pound, thirteen-ounce little girl we named Brittany Danielle. She was fairly healthy but had to be transported to the newborn intensive care unit (NICU) because her body temperature wouldn't drop below 104°. Doctors were worried about a serious infection.

I got to hold her for less than five minutes because they wanted to get her to the NICU. At 3:00 AM, I got to see my little girl but couldn't hold her yet. They wanted to finish running some tests to make sure she was healthy. I took a good look at her and went back to my room to get some sleep.

As soon as I woke up, I asked to go see my little girl. I was heartbroken when I was told I still couldn't hold her. I considered myself lucky because she wasn't as sick as the other babies in the NICU. The only machine she was hooked up to was an IV for fluids and antibiotics. There were so many babies in the NICU, but none as bad off as the baby in the incubator beside Brittany. This baby was so tiny she would fit in the palm of my hand. Her parents weren't allowed to touch her.

The next day my prayers were answered. Her tests came back clean. She had to stay on the antibiotics and in the hospital NICU, but at least I could hold her. When I picked her up and snuggled her to me, I fell so deeply in love with this little angel. My little angel. My baby girl.

I never knew that I could love another human being so much, but she completely stole my heart. I didn't want to put her down. I wanted to hold her forever. I knew I couldn't stay in NICU that long because it wasn't healthy for the other babies. The parents were limited to being there only during visiting hours for the health of the babies. It was hard being a new parent and not being able to spend every waking minute with my newborn baby.

The last night Brittany was in the NICU, I was holding her when a nurse came in and said it was time for her evening feeding. The couple with the tiny infant girl was staring at me and Brittany. I felt so sorry for the mom because I knew what she was going through. It was hard having a baby she couldn't hold, let alone touch. I wondered when she looked at me if she was happy for me or jealous.

When the nurse brought me the bottle, I asked the mother of the little baby if she'd like to feed Brittany. Tears welled up in her eyes. "You would really let me do that?" she asked.

I said, "Yes." I stood up and she came over and sat down in the rocker. I kissed Brittany on the forehead and handed her over to a stranger, but one I knew I could trust. This stranger wanted nothing more than to hold her baby girl, but she took solace in holding mine.

Brittany became the center of my universe; my life revolved around her. I was in love again, but this was the first time that I knew what unconditional love was supposed to feel like. I spent every waking moment with this little blonde-haired, green-eyed girl. She was witty and smart and loved being outside in the backyard. Her laughter was contagious, and we spent hours laughing with each other while playing silly games.

When she was four years old, her father and I divorced, and I've raised her by myself since then. After our divorce, Brittany never spent much time with her dad, so she didn't really get to know him. It's hard to get to know someone when you're four and you see him every other weekend. Over the years Brittany and I became inseparable. This was why it was going to be so difficult to tell her that I had cancer. My daughter, my baby girl, the love of my life was only twelve. How could I tell her the only parent she's ever really known has breast cancer and could possibly die?

Die. Oh, my God. I wouldn't be there when she started high school. She'd go on her first date without my being there to make sure her hair was fixed just right or to give the guy a hard time. I wouldn't be around to help heal her first broken heart. I'd miss that day when she came home with that beautiful twinkle in her eye, having fallen madly in love.

Love. I wouldn't be there to help her pick out her wedding dress. I wouldn't be there to ease her fears when she started to get cold feet about getting married. I wouldn't be there to help her get dressed or to give her something old or something new. I wouldn't get to see my baby girl walk down the aisle and marry the man of her dreams.

Dreams. I wouldn't be around to help her make her dreams come true. I wouldn't be there to encourage her and continually tell her she could do anything she wanted. I've always encouraged her to follow her heart. I've always told her she could do anything she wanted. I have told her that the word *can't* is not a part of our vocabulary. I've told her that since she was a baby.

Babies. I wouldn't be around to see my baby have babies. I wouldn't get to hold my first grandchild. I wouldn't get to spoil my grandchildren and send them home. Would she tell them about me? Would she show them pictures of us together? Would she remember my birthday or be sad at Christmas?

After what seemed like an eternity of silence, Dr. Crawford said I should go home and try to have a good weekend. Have a good weekend? How in the world was I supposed to do that? He said he would like to see me back at the clinic on Monday, so he made me a follow-up appointment. As I made my way to the door, he put his hand on my shoulder and said, "I'm sorry." He said it was going to be okay and we would discuss options on Monday.

As I walked back down the long hallway, I tried not to think about what I had just learned. I just wanted out of the hospital. I walked past a few other waiting rooms, where I felt as if people were staring at me like I was stark naked. Did they know I had cancer? Was I looking different? Did I smell different? What were they staring at?

I just needed to get out of there, so I started walking a little faster. The faster I walked, the further away the door seemed. It was as if the floor had turned into a moving walkway going in the opposite direction. The door got smaller and smaller, and now the walls were starting to close in on me. What was happening to me? My heart started pounding, and I broke out in a cold sweat. Now people were really staring at me. Before I knew it, I was in a full force run and busted out of the emergency room doors as if being chased. I couldn't tell you if I ran anybody over or knocked anybody down on my way out. At that point, I honestly didn't care.

I had to get to my car before I passed out. I was shaking so bad I couldn't walk. My legs were like Jell-O, and nothing was making any sense. When I reached the car, I just stood there, leaning against it. What would I do next? Where would I turn? All sorts of thoughts ran through my mind, but the one that kept coming back was: *How do I tell my daughter?*

Chapter 7

Telling My Loved Ones

Telling my loved ones was harder than hearing the words myself. I hoped that if I never said the words out loud, then they wouldn't be true. I thought about not telling my friends and family, but I knew those close to me would eventually figure it out. I knew I had to tell them, but how? Should I just blurt it out, or break it to them gently? I guess it didn't matter how I told them as long as I told them, and I knew I had to tell them.

My Family

I had to tell Brittany, but she was still in class. I needed to call Vickie because I knew she would be worried. It had been over an hour since my scheduled appointment time. I was surprised she hadn't called me already, but I knew she was probably very busy. Vickie had a very important job on the base. She was the four-star general's right-hand man, so to speak. Her title was Command Chief Master Sergeant, and people were always wanting some of her time. I often felt I had to make an appointment with her just to spend some quality family time.

Vickie was very well respected and popular—too popular for me, in fact. We couldn't have lunch together without someone coming up and wanting to talk to her about work or something. I found this unacceptable, but she reminded me on many occasions that this was her job and she had to be accessible for the enlisted personnel.

The bad thing about her popularity was that I lost my own identity. After people learned we were sisters, I was no longer "Kim." Instead, I was always referred to as "Chief's sister." I hated that. One time someone asked me, "Hey, aren't you the Chief's sister?"

"No", I said.

The person stared at me for a few seconds and then said, "I'm sorry, but I'm sure I met you at a function the other day and she introduced you as her sister."

"I'm Kim first, Chief's sister second." The person looked at me as if I were crazy. He was partially right.

Even though this bothered me at times, I was proud of her and proud to be her sister. She was admired by so many people and had accomplished so much in the Air Force during her career. Being her sister also gave me a few perks: recognition at ceremonies and invitations to parties and high-profile events. But, in all fairness and respect to her, Vickie was my rock during my cancer battle.

As I mentioned earlier, Vickie left home when I was only eight years old, so I didn't really know her until I moved in with her when I was nineteen. We had so much fun living together. One of the funniest things she learned about me happened when we were out to dinner one evening. I don't remember the name of the restaurant, but it was a buffet inside a mall in Aurora, Colorado. This particular day the restaurant was fairly crowded. We got our food and sat down at a table in the center of the place—my choice, of course.

Our conversation was fairly normal when I suddenly asked Vickie if she had ever seen me eat like a baby. She chuckled and said no. I continued to eat but pretended that I had gotten choked and started coughing kind of loud. People were starting to look at me, and I noticed Vickie was staring at me too.

"What?" I asked.

"You asked me if I had seen you eat like a baby. Are you going to show me or what?"

I just smiled and looked around to see how many people were looking at me. I continued to look around while coughing and said, "Oh, yeah, I forgot."

I immediately stuck my hand in my mashed potatoes and gravy, scooped up a handful and smeared it from one side of my face to the other. With gravy dripping from my chin, I looked at her, smiled, and said, "That's how I eat like a baby." The look on my sister's face at that moment was priceless!

Another funny moment while living with my sister was when she took advantage of my extreme fear of bugs. I'm afraid of just about any type of bug, especially spiders and grasshoppers. This particular day involved a poor, helpless grasshopper.

We were sitting out back on her patio when she came strolling over to me with a shit-eating grin on her face. I knew something was up, so I eased up out of my chair and headed toward the door. It was at that time she dangled Mr. Grasshopper in front of my face.

Shrieking, I ran inside and down to the basement level and hid in the closet. When she came down and ran past me, I jumped out and ran upstairs to the top level, where there were three bedrooms. I went in one bedroom while she ran into another.

At that point I decided to head back downstairs and out the front door so I could keep on running down the street if I had to. As I hit the stairs, Vickie was right on my tail with Mr. Grasshopper in her hand. By this time the grasshopper was tired and upset. I could swear he was making a growling noise, growing fangs, and dripping gobs of saliva just like Cujo. I had to get out of the house and away from that rabid grasshopper.

I gained strength and hit the bottom of the stairs, picking up speed as I headed for the front door. I was moving fast when I hit the latch on the door handle to get it open. Now here's where it gets interesting … the door was locked.

I slammed full force into the door with my sister and the demonic grasshopper right on my heels. I'm sure I don't need to draw you a picture of what happened next. My sister slammed full force into me, which pushed me further into the door.

We fell to the floor in fits of laughter until a thought entered my mind—the grasshopper. I jumped up and got away from her as quick as I could. I'd like to make the statement here that no animals were harmed during the run through the house, but it should be pretty obvious what happened to poor Mr. Grasshopper.

Vickie and I had fun together, but we also weathered some tough times. We were together when our grandmother died in 1986. Vickie nursed me back to health when I was in a really bad car accident that same year. We made the drive from Colorado back to West Virginia when our mom died in January 1991. Mom's death was hard on me because we were really close, but Vickie was there for me the entire time. She helped me through my divorce, and I always turned to her when I needed advice about the military.

As I kept trying to dial her number on my cell phone, I couldn't stop thinking about her and how close we had become since we both got stationed in Germany. While I was living with Vickie, she learned so much about me and who I was. She learned I wasn't afraid to have fun and be myself. She learned I loved to laugh. She learned I had fears. Most important, she learned I loved her and needed her.

So there I stood at my car, with my phone in my trembling hands. A few people stopped to ask me if I was all right. Not really, I replied, but I thanked them for their concern. I finally dialed my sister's number at work, and her assistant answered the phone. She told me Vickie was in a meeting and asked if she could pass on a message. At that moment she must have remembered why I was calling. She asked if she needed to interrupt her, and I said yes. She was silent for a few seconds and then quietly said, "I'm so sorry."

It wasn't until Vickie got on the phone that I broke down for the first time. She said, "Honey, what's wrong?"

I couldn't talk, but finally managed to say, "Vickie, it's cancer. I have cancer."

"Kim, I'm so sorry." As she was talking, I was just crying and looking at the sky, still wondering how I was going to tell Brittany. She told me to go home, and she'd meet me there. At that point, my tears turned to anger.

"No!" I said. "I'm in the military and I have a job to do. I have to get back to work."

Knowing how stubborn I was, she said if I was going back to work, she would like me to stop by her office first. I agreed. She said, "I love you, Sis," and hung up. I got in my car and headed back to work. On my way back to work, I called my other sister, Lori. This was an extremely difficult call because Lori and I were still as close as we were growing up. We talked every day on the phone, and this day was no exception.

When she answered, I tried to make small talk, but I couldn't keep it together. I said, "Lori, my biopsy came back, and it's cancer. I have breast cancer." I started crying and so did she. Neither one of us could talk, so I told her I would call her back later that night. I also asked her to call our brother, Roger, and tell him because I didn't think I could make another call. Lori was having an extremely difficult time accepting this, but I think it had a little to do with the fact that our dad had just died in August. Here it was December, and I was giving her more bad news.

The drive back to work took forever, and I don't remember most of the trip. I got to the base and drove to my office the long way around because I wasn't ready to face anyone. I drove around a few more minutes and decided I had better get to my sister's office before she sent out a search party. Without further hesitation, I parked and went inside.

Vickie worked on the second floor of her building, and the climb up the stairs was terrible. I was emotionally drained at that moment and felt as if my shoes were filled with cement. I made it to her office, where she was waiting with open arms. I fell into her arms and stayed there while we cried together. We sat down on the couch in her office and didn't say a word. I turned to her and asked her how I was going to tell Brittany. She said to just be honest, and if I wanted her to, she would tell her or be with me when I did it.

We talked a little more, and she asked me if I had called Lori. I said yes, but that I had to call her back. After a few minutes I told her I needed to get back to work. She then told me she had called my commander, and he told her to tell me to go home. I couldn't go home because I would just sit there and feel sorry for myself, and I wasn't ready for that. I didn't want to have those feelings yet because I was still mad at cancer. I was mad because this disease had invaded my body and could destroy my life and my family. I was mad because I didn't have a say-so in the matter. I was just downright mad.

I stood up and hugged her and told her I would call her later. I walked back across the parking lot to my office, but I didn't want to go inside. I finally worked up the courage and opened the door.

Friends and Coworkers

When I walked inside, I felt as if I were walking into a confined space with no air. My chest felt like it was caving in and the life was being sucked out of my body a little at a time. My commander was at lunch, as was my best friend, George, which was a good thing. George was older than I was and was not known for his friendliness or pleasing personality. He was rough around the edges but had a sweet, old soul. When I first met him, I didn't like him and couldn't get past his grumpy mood. He was a tall, stocky man with salt-and-pepper hair. I rarely saw a smile on his face, but when I did, it would melt my heart. His eyes sparkled and he had a deep belly laugh, sort of like Santa Claus.

I consider myself a friendly and happy person (sometimes too happy), so you can imagine how well we got along at first. I would go to work in the morning and George would already be there. I would walk in and say, "Good morning, George." The response I got was something that sounded like a low growl from a pissed-off dog. Throughout the day I would try to make small talk but was always met with the same growl. I guess he figured I would eventually give up. However, George didn't know me very well.

This routine continued for about a month until I decided to deploy a different tactic. One morning when I came in, I stood beside his desk and repeated, "Good morning, George," about ten times. Finally, he looked over his glasses and said, "Good morning, little girl."

"Little girl" was the nickname I earned from him, and it became one of my favorite things about our friendship. He gave me the nickname either because I was younger than he was, or because I acted like a little girl. I didn't care what the reason was because I liked the nickname and I liked our friendship.

I guess I changed George, or he was just trying to keep me from running my mouth, because the next morning when I walked in the office I was greeted with a smile and a "Good Morning, little girl." Damn. I didn't even get the first word in this time. I was smiling to myself and thinking, *Yeah, I got him to change.* He was smiling to himself and thinking, *Yeah, I got her to shut up.*

George was truly my best friend, and I don't think I could have handled seeing him as soon as I got to the office, so I'm glad he was still at lunch. I went to my desk to put my stuff down and headed straight for the bathroom. I locked the door and after doing my business, washed my hands and splashed water on my face. I couldn't look at myself in the mirror because I didn't want to see what I looked like. I didn't want to see my red, puffy eyes or the fact that my face no longer had color. Besides, if I looked in the mirror I would see the sadness and fear in my face and would start crying again. Or I'd punch the mirror, and I certainly didn't want to do that either. I composed myself and tried to keep from throwing up. I succeeded, took a deep breath, and left the bathroom.

Another friend of mine sat directly across from the bathroom entrance. She must have seen me go in because she was waiting when I came out. When she initially found out I was having a biopsy, she told me about her niece who had battled breast cancer. The first thing she asked was, "Did you get your test results yet?"

"Yes, I just got back from the doctor and unfortunately, it's not good news." She came toward me, but I held up my hand, stopping her in her tracks.

"I'm sorry," she said.

"Thank you, but I don't want to talk about this right now." I turned and went back to my office, where I sat down to try to do some work. I couldn't concentrate, so I decided to just read some emails. That didn't work either. Then it occurred to me I hadn't had anything to eat since breakfast. I went to the vending machine to get a healthy snack because I didn't want to get cancer from eating junk food. *Oh, wait, too late for that.* So I headed back to my desk with peanut butter crackers, a Snickers, M & M's, and a Pepsi. I nibbled at the crackers, but no matter how hard I tried, I couldn't get them down. I tried the candy bar and M & M's, but I couldn't get them down either. I threw everything away and decided to head out for a walk.

On my way out of the building, I ran into a few people who had already heard the news. I guess when Vickie had called my commander, he must have told a few people, who told a few other people. The problem was that each time the news was told to someone, it changed. I went from having breast cancer to brain cancer to some other type of cancer to being terminal to being contagious.

Contagious? How was that even possible? I wasn't mad at the people passing on the news or at my commander or my sister. I was still mad at the fact I had cancer and was pissed off at the cancer itself. I walked around the parking lot a few times to clear my head and finally went back to work. I was able to sit and read emails for a while and get some work done, but I kept being disturbed by people's looks and whispers.

That was it! I went to the commander and asked him if we could pull everyone together in his office so we could tell them all at once. He asked me if I was sure I wanted to do this. "Yes," I said. I explained how people were already talking and whispering, and that they deserved to know the truth. Then he asked me if I was going to be able to do it. "Hell, no," I sort of chuckled. "My sister is going to come over and do it because I won't be able to." He agreed with me. That was the first time I laughed since I had learned of my cancer diagnosis that morning.

When Vickie got to my office, the secretary did an overhead page and asked everyone to come to the commander's office for an important meeting. At this time only a few had known the truth, but George hadn't been told yet because he was still at lunch. He had no idea what was happening to me. Just as people were going into the commander's office, George came in and joined everyone else.

Before Vickie and I went in, she asked me what I wanted her to tell everyone and what was the most important thing I wanted them to know. I told her to be honest about my cancer and stress that they should not treat me any differently. I said I'm still the same person I was when I left the building this morning, and I didn't want to be treated with kid gloves. I'm still me.

We walked in, and as Vickie made her way to the front of the office, I stopped right by the door. I didn't know if I was ready to hear it all again, and I wanted to be by the door just in case I had to make a mad dash outside. The people who already knew what was going on looked at me with sympathy. I couldn't look at anyone other than Vickie.

She started by telling them I had a biopsy on Monday of a suspicious lump in my breast. Then she told them I had received the results this morning and the news wasn't good. Her voice was quivering a little when she said, "Kim was diagnosed with breast cancer this morning." There was a large, collective gasp around the room. That did it. The tears began to flow.

A coworker was sitting in the chair by the door. He must have sensed my desire to flee because he reached up, grabbed my hand, and squeezed. At this point, I looked over at George, who stood with his head down. He couldn't, or maybe wouldn't, look at me.

Vickie continued through tears, saying that we didn't know anything specific about the cancer other than that I had it. She said I was facing more appointments, surgery, and who knows what else, but we would find out more when I went back to the doctor on Monday. In the meantime, per my request, she asked them to not treat me any differently and to continue to give me a hard time like always. That comment got a small chuckle from everyone and lightened the mood just a little. Vickie thanked everyone for coming and asked them to remember me and Brittany and the rest of my family in their prayers.

As people filtered out of the office, they stopped to hug me and give me words of encouragement. It was hard to stand there and listen to what people were saying without screaming. I wanted to scream because they had no idea what I was thinking or feeling. They had no idea that I didn't want their hugs or words of encouragement just then. I was mad. It wasn't fair. I was too young, and more important, I felt as if I had lost control of my life. I hated feeling like that.

After everyone left, my commander asked if there was anything he could do. All I had to do was ask. *Okay,* I thought to myself. *I'll ask even if the questions are only in my head. Can you take away my cancer? Can you make it so that when I tell my daughter she understands and is not scared? Can you make the next few months as painless and worry-free as possible?* I thanked him for the gesture and went back to my office.

George was waiting in the office that we shared. I thought my friend was unbreakable—at least I did until he learned I had cancer. He didn't say much, but I noticed him looking at me from time to time. When I would catch his eye, he would look away. The afternoon went on, with neither of us saying anything. At times, I wanted to burp or fart just to make some noise and make him laugh.

His silence hurt me, but I could understand why he was acting this way. He didn't know what to say or, more important, how to say it, so he said nothing. Late in the afternoon he got up, shut down his computer, and said he needed to go home. He asked me if I was going to be at work on Monday, and I said yes. I explained that I had to return to the doctor first thing Monday morning, but I would be in after that. Without looking at me, he said he would see me Monday and left.

I looked at the clock. It was almost 4:00 PM, time to leave to go to the retirement ceremony. I called Vickie and asked if she was ready to go and if she could drive. We made plans for me to park my car at home and then hop in her car and ride with her. I left work and walked to my car, as if I were heading in no direction at all. I was a walking zombie. I drove home and sat in the car until Vickie got there to pick me up. I wasn't ready to go upstairs and face Brittany, and besides, she knew I wouldn't be home until around 6:00.

Vickie showed up, and I got into her car to head to the retirement ceremony. Before we drove off, she asked me if I was sure I wanted to go, considering what I had just found out. Yes, I said. Cancer is not going to change how I live my life. Yes, I might have to make a few alterations, but I wasn't going to change.

> *Even though my mom was gone, I knew that just having her arms around me or talking to me would take some of the pain away.*

The drive there seemed like it took hours. It was fairly quiet, with neither one of us talking about anything important. What do you say in a situation like that? We talked about how cold it was getting and if it was going to snow. Then silence again.

As if she knew what I was thinking, Vickie said, "This is one of those times where you wish Mom were still alive, isn't it?" I sat there in silence and let the tears flow down my cheeks. She was right. I wanted my mom so bad right then. I knew she wouldn't have been able to change the fact that I had cancer. I knew she couldn't have spared me from everything that was about to happen in my life. However, I knew that hearing Mom's voice would have taken away some of the pain. She would have comforted me with her words. I knew if I could have been in her loving arms at that moment my heart would not be breaking. She would have told me to be brave and strong. She would have told me to pray and ask God for his help and to give me strength to get through all this. I knew she was in heaven watching down on me. But most of all, even though she was gone, I knew she loved me.

We pulled into the parking lot where the retirement ceremony was being held. Vickie said it wasn't too late to change my mind. I thought about it, but I had to be there to support my friend, Shelly, and her husband on this special day. We walked in and took a seat in the last row. I didn't want to be too close to the front because I didn't want anyone to notice I had been crying.

One of my friends noticed something because she came up to me afterwards and asked if I was okay. I told her no. I took her by the hand, and we walked to another room that was empty. I told her I had cancer. She grabbed me and hugged me. She said she was so sorry and if there was anything she could do, all I had to do was ask. I asked her if she could go find Vickie for me because I felt like I was about to pass out. Vickie came in and asked if I was okay. I said I was feeling a little overwhelmed and told her I wanted to go home. She said Shelly was looking for me and wanted to know what she should tell her.

About that time Shelly came in and realized I had been crying. She asked what was wrong. I told her the news, and she started crying. She couldn't believe I had just found out I had cancer but still came to her husband's retirement ceremony. I told her she was my friend and I wouldn't miss this for anything.

Her husband came in to find her and wondered what we all were doing hiding in the back room. She told him the news, and we all just stood there and hugged and cried. Somebody went and got the minister who had been at the retirement ceremony and brought him in. We talked for a few minutes, and then we all gathered hands and prayed. I broke down because prayer has always been a crucial part of my life, and that was exactly what I needed at that moment.

We stood around and talked for a while, but I knew I had to get home and face my daughter. She had a dance to go to, and I promised her I would be home before she left. I kept going over in my head what I would say to her and how I would tell her, but no matter how many times I practiced saying it, I was certain it would not come out the way I wanted it to.

Vickie and I talked on the way home about the retirement ceremony and again about how cold it was getting. We talked about our plans for the weekend and what we were doing for Christmas. We talked about the Christmas markets and which ones we were going to visit. We talked about almost everything, but we didn't talk about cancer. I was going to be doing that enough tonight.

Brittany

We pulled up in front of our apartment building, and I thought I was going to have a full-blown panic attack. I couldn't bring myself to open the door. I finally got out of the car, and Vickie asked me one more time if I wanted her to go in with me. I said, "No, I have to do this by myself. She needs to hear it from me. I'll be fine." We hugged, and I walked away feeling overwhelmed and about ready to pass out.

I walked into the stairwell and started climbing the stairs to the fourth floor. I took my time, trying to breathe as calmly as I could. I stood outside my doorway for a few minutes to gather my composure before going in. I opened the door and expected Brittany to meet me, but she didn't. I took off my coat and hung it up. I yelled out, "Hey, baby girl, I'm home!" (I still do this to this day).

"Hey, Mommy, I'm in the kitchen."

I walked into the kitchen where my baby girl, just twelve years old and so beautiful, was sitting at the kitchen table working on a thousand-piece jigsaw puzzle. This is a Christmas tradition that we started when she was about seven years old.

I buy a jigsaw puzzle every year around Thanksgiving that is at least a thousand pieces. On December 1, we open it and start working on it. Our goal is to have it finished before Christmas, and then we glue it together and hang it up until after the first of the year. Then we take it down and throw it away or donate it to a thrift store.

When I walked into the kitchen, Brittany looked at me and said, "Mom, news?"

"No, baby, Mommy doesn't want to watch the news right now."

She once again said, "Mom, news?"

"Do you want to watch the news, baby girl?"

She looked at me somewhat frustrated and said, "Mom! What was the doctor's news?"

I let out a huge sigh. "Baby girl, Mommy has cancer, but we'll be okay. Everything will be just fine."

Wow! That was easier than I thought it would be. I was waiting for her to scream or cry or shout. But nothing. She didn't even look at me. That hurt me. I was sad and mad that she wasn't reacting like I thought she would, or like *I* thought she should. Did she not care? Did she not love me? All she said was, "Does this mean I can't go to my dance now?"

"Absolutely not! I may have cancer but that doesn't mean it's going to change our lives or in the way we live it. Go to the dance and have fun."

I wanted her to go and have fun, but mainly, I wanted her out of the house so I could have some time to put things in perspective. I wanted to be alone because all day long people had been around me. I wanted to be alone without anybody asking me if I was okay, but I didn't want to tell her that.

She left to get dressed. I went and changed clothes because I had to get out of the uniform I had been wearing all day. It smelled like the hospital, and what I truly wanted to do was burn it. Knowing I couldn't do that, I decided to throw my clothes in the washer.

Brittany's friend rang the doorbell and asked if she was ready. She came out of her room and hugged me good-bye. I told her to have fun and that I would see her later. She left and I was somewhat relieved. I had the house to myself so I could cry, and boy, did I need to cry. It had to come out. I set my kitchen timer for fifteen minutes because that's all the time I was going to allow myself to cry. After that, no more crying.

I walked around my apartment as if I were seeing it for the first time. I walked into the kitchen and opened the refrigerator, and it hit me again that I hadn't had anything to eat. Everything I looked at wasn't appealing, and most brought on the gag reflex. I decided on a chicken pot pie—comfort food.

I put the pot pie in the oven and my phone rang. I didn't want to answer it, but I knew Brittany was out and was afraid something might be wrong. It was my commander. He was just checking on me to make sure I was doing all right and to see if I needed anything. I told him I was fine and that I was getting ready to eat something. He asked how Brittany took the news and I said surprisingly well. He said good night and bid me a good weekend.

While waiting for my pot pie to bake, I called some close friends and gave them the news. Everyone was shocked and couldn't believe what they were hearing. They were no more shocked than I was, of course, but it was good to have everyone know. News travels fast, especially bad news, and I wanted my friends to hear it from me.

I picked at my dinner and tried watching a little television, but I couldn't concentrate, so I decided to take my dog, Hannah, out for a walk. Hannah is a Yorkie and cute as a button. She came from a breeder in Belgium, and we drove to "just look" at her; but she was so tiny and cute we couldn't say no. We brought her home the same night and became totally crazy about her. I bought her for Brittany as a birthday present, but she became my dog and was never far from my side.

When we got ready to go out for a walk, she was acting as if she had lost her best friend. She wasn't wagging her tail or being her bouncy self. She must have known something was wrong because during our walk, she would walk alongside me and look up at me with her big, brown eyes. It was too cold to stay out long, so we came back in and I put her on my lap. I held her close and told her I had cancer but that it would be okay. I thanked her for being there to listen to me whenever I needed to talk. Hannah started licking my chin, so I nuzzled her close until my phone rang again.

This time it was Vickie checking on me to see how things went with Brittany and to make sure I had eaten. I told her things went well and yes, I picked at my food. We were in the middle of talking when I heard Brittany's keys in the door. I told Vickie I had to go. She told me she loved me and would call me tomorrow.

I asked Brittany if she had a good time and she just nodded. She also said she was tired so she was just going to go to bed. I told her that was fine, so she went to brush her teeth and put on her pajamas. She came in and told me she was finished and ready for bed. I told her I would come to tuck her in, but she stopped when she was almost at her door and said, "Mom, I'm getting too old for you to tuck me in now."

I turned and looked at Brittany. "Oh, okay. Then at least come and give me a hug and a kiss good night." She started toward me but stopped again.

"Mom, I'm getting too old for that too."

Choking back tears I said, "Okay, baby girl, I'll see you in the morning. Sleep tight. I love you."

"Love you, too," she said and went into her room and closed the door.

Before cancer, Brittany always wanted me to tuck her in, sit on her bed for a while, and talk to her while she was falling asleep. Before cancer, Brittany would never go to bed without a hug and a kiss from me. Before cancer, Brittany never slept with her door closed. But all that changed, when cancer entered our lives.

I felt like I had been sucker punched. My gut was aching and I was fighting back tears. I was hurt, and I wanted to rush right into Brittany's room and tell her how I was feeling, but I wasn't sure how to do it or even if I should do it. Maybe I should just go to bed and deal with it in the morning.

I took a hot shower and realized how exhausted I was. I was so tired that I almost passed out under the steam of hot water. The water felt good, so I sat down in the tub and started crying again. I had vowed not to cry anymore, but I couldn't help it. The tears flowed freely. After a few minutes I got out of the shower, wrapped a towel around myself, went to my room, and closed the door. I dressed and climbed into my bed, hoping that sleep would soon follow.

I looked over at the clock, and it was almost midnight. *Gee, I've had cancer for almost fourteen hours now. Well, I've probably had it longer, but I have only known about it for fourteen hours.* Was it growing faster and taking over my body? Was it coursing through my veins with each beat of my heart? Had it already invaded one of my vital organs?

"Stop it, Kim," I said to myself. "Shut up and go to sleep." I needed to find a way to turn my brain off and fall asleep. I needed the rest now more than ever. I tried counting sheep. I tried reading. I tried watching television. I tossed and turned, but nothing worked. Then I tried praying. Within minutes I was sound asleep, because the next thing I knew, the sun was shining through the cracks of my blinds.

I turned over and checked the clock. It was 9:00 AM. That must be wrong, because Brittany normally would wake me up by now, or at least crawl in bed with me. I sat up in bed. It was quiet, so I figured she must have slept in also.

I got up and opened my bedroom door. Brittany's door was open, and the living room door was closed. *That's odd*, I thought. I opened that door and saw Brittany lying on the couch watching a movie. I went over to her and rubbed her on the head and said good morning.

She looked up at me and said, "Good morning, Mom." I asked her why the door was closed and why she didn't wake me up. She said she didn't want to bother me. I told her it was okay and her routine was the one thing I loved about Saturday morning, but she didn't respond.

I made my way to the kitchen to get some breakfast because I was starving. After all, it had been almost twenty-four hours with hardly any food. I asked Brittany what she would like, and she said she had made some cereal for herself, so she wasn't hungry. *Great, breakfast alone.*

Brittany didn't have much to say to me or do with me that weekend. She spent a great deal of time with her friends or in her room, watching television or a movie. I got really upset because I felt she had turned her back on me. It seemed like she didn't care. How could she do this to me? I have done so much for her. *If this keeps up*, I thought, *it will kill me long before the cancer ever does.*

I don't recall the rest of the weekend, and I don't even remember if we went to church. What I do know is that my phone rang off the hook, as did my doorbell, with friends wanting to see how I was doing. Most of the time I let the answering machine pick up and didn't answer the door. I didn't think that exposing Brittany to any more of this cancer talk would be beneficial to either one of us, so I shut out everyone.

Cancer was doing what I said it wouldn't do—change my life. Before, I never would have let my answering machine pick up if I was home, and I never would have let someone ring my doorbell without answering it.

Chapter 8

My Options

Sunday night came, and I knew in the morning I would learn a little more about my cancer and what my options were. I went to bed and spent a somewhat restless night wondering what the doctor would have to say. I had asked Vickie earlier that day if she would go with me to the doctor. I wanted to make sure I understood everything the doctor was saying and to ask questions on the things we didn't understand. She said she wouldn't let me go alone even if I wanted to.

Monday morning finally came, but I had only slept for about three hours before my alarm clock went off. I went through the normal routine: shower, breakfast, and helping Brittany get things ready so she could get out the door to school. She was still somewhat quiet and didn't talk much, and I was trying to leave her alone and give her some space.

I went to work first because my appointment wasn't until around 10:00. One of the first things I did when I got to work was to call Brittany's school and talk to her counselors. I wanted to let them know about my cancer because I was afraid it would affect her in school. After all, she was already acting differently at home, so I wanted to be sure they knew the reason for her possible change in behavior and academic performance.

When it was time to go, Vickie drove because I was sure I would be too upset to drive back. Our mood was fairly calm, but we both figured the situation was going to get somewhat upsetting later. We parked and took the long walk down the hall to the General Surgery Clinic. I checked in at the front desk, and we were asked to have a seat in the waiting room.

We took a seat toward the back of the room, taking inventory of who was there. The others were all women—ten women, to be exact. The television was on, and some of the women were watching it, while others were reading. Everyone seemed to notice that there were only women around, especially when a certain commercial came on.

The commercial I'm referring to was about breast cancer and statistics. The commercial started out, "One in every eight women will be diagnosed with breast cancer." Some of the women looked around the room as if to count the others and figure out who was going to be the one. I saved them the trouble. I said, "Don't worry, ladies. I'm the one." They didn't say anything and looked somewhat appalled that I had even opened my mouth. It wasn't the first time, and as long as I'm alive, it won't be the last.

Lucky for them—or maybe lucky for me—we were called back into the doctor's office. Vickie and I laughed at the women's reaction on my way to the doctor's office. She knew all too well that I didn't know when to keep my mouth shut.

When we walked into the office, I was greeted by Dr. Crawford and another doctor who was introduced as the plastic surgeon. He took my vitals, and then we all sat down to have a chat. The first thing the general surgeon asked was, "How was your weekend?"

"How was my weekend?" I laughed. "Let's see. On Friday, you turned my world upside down. On Saturday and Sunday, I spent the entire weekend in my apartment with my daughter, who turned into a complete stranger. I felt like throwing up most of the weekend. I haven't eaten enough to keep a bird alive, and now I'm here getting ready to talk to you about surgery options for my cancer. How do you think my weekend went?"

He had no response. I continued, "Doc, I can handle the cancer diagnosis. Bring it on. I'm ready to fight. However, what I can't handle is my twelve-year-old daughter turning her back on me!"

He took my hand and said, "Kim, she's twelve. The only thing she knows about cancer is it could kill you. She probably figures if she stops loving you right now, then it won't hurt so bad if you die. Give her some time and some space. She'll be fine."

I was now crying, and I swore to myself I wasn't going to cry today. Damn him.

We started talking about cancer and surgery and options. I almost felt as if I were having another out-of-body experience. It seemed like we were talking about somebody else. Unfortunately, we were talking about me. I was presented with a few options for surgery: (1) a lumpectomy with options; (2) a mastectomy with no reconstruction; (3) a mastectomy with immediate reconstruction. I couldn't believe I had surgical options.

> *Clean margins means that the complete edge of a tumor has no cancer cells.*

With option one, the lumpectomy, surgeons could remove the cancerous tumor, run it to pathology, and see if it had clean margins. Clean margins would mean that the complete edge of the tumor was clean, with no cancer cells. If it had clean margins, then I would be sewn up and the surgery would be over. If the margins were not clean, then they would come back in and either take a larger chunk or remove the entire breast (mastectomy) at that time.

The problem with option one was I didn't know how I would wake up. I would either wake up with my left breast still in place and a large cut on it, or I would wake up without my breast and an implant in its place. I wanted to *know* how I was going to wake up. Scratch option one.

Option two was a modified radical mastectomy with no reconstruction. This procedure removes the entire breast, including the nipple and areola and underarm lymph nodes, but saves the chest muscles. There would be no reconstruction, and I would be missing my left breast. I liked this option because there would be no question whether the surgeons got all the cancer. However, I was young and didn't want to walk around without a breast. Scratch option number two.

Option three was the same as option two but with reconstruction. The surgeons could do the reconstruction with an implant, either saline or silicon, or they could do a procedure known as a TRAM flap. TRAM is an acronym for transverse rectus abdominis myocutaneous. This procedure removes the skin, muscle, and fat from a woman's abdomen and relocates it to her breast. The option using the implant would be quick and fairly simple, but it would place a foreign object in my body. The TRAM flap procedure would take longer and require a longer and harder recovery, but it would use my tissue and thus be all natural.

After Dr. Crawford presented the options, my head was swimming. Vickie was asking questions, but I had no idea what to ask or what to say. He recommended a lumpectomy because I was young and might feel more comfortable just having the lump removed instead of my entire breast. He said because I was single, I might meet someone and would feel more comfortable having both my real breasts. I told him if I met a guy and he was only worried about whether or not I have real breasts or any breasts at all, for that matter, then he wasn't the guy for me.

Dr. Crawford looked at me and asked what option I would prefer. "I need to decide now?" I asked.

"The sooner the better," he said. They needed a decision because they had to get the surgery scheduled and would need to order the implant if that is what I chose. Order the implant? I never would have imagined that I would be ordering my breast from a catalog.

Dr. Crawford also said they would have to do a little surgery on the right breast to make it "match" the left in size and shape after surgery. I told him I honestly didn't know what I wanted to do and that I needed to think about it. He said that was fine, but he would call me on Wednesday to get my decision. I agreed to that.

We talked a little more about my cancer, but he didn't know much. All we knew for sure was that it was breast cancer. We didn't know the size of the tumor or anything else, and we wouldn't know the rest until after the surgery.

Surgery. I was scared to death just thinking about it. We scheduled it for Monday, December 17. I had a week to prepare for what I was about to face. He asked that I come back into the hospital on Friday morning to do all my pre-op paperwork, blood tests, and X-rays.

He got everything scheduled and asked if I had any questions. I wanted to ask if he was sure it was cancer. I wanted to ask if he was sure they didn't mix up my biopsy results with someone else's. I wanted to ask if he thought it had spread. I wanted to ask if I was going to die. But I didn't.

Instead, I shook his hand and told him I'd talk to him on

Wednesday. We left and drove back to the base. Our talk was mainly on my options. I told Vickie that I wanted the mastectomy even though the doctor recommended I have a lumpectomy, but I didn't want to have the TRAM flap done because I needed to recover quickly. It was important for me to get back to normal as soon as possible because I wanted Brittany to see me as normal again. She needed me to be better soon, and I needed to be better for her. Vickie agreed with me, and then we changed the subject.

Upon returning to work, I went in and talked to my commander about my surgery. I told him it was going to be next Monday and that I would have a few things that I needed to take care of as far as medical appointments, but otherwise, I would be at work. He said I could take that week off, but I thanked him and turned it down. I had to keep myself busy.

There was one thing I asked of him. Would he mind sending out an email to everyone in our region letting them know what was going on with me? In my job, I was responsible for the management of logistics programs for more than twenty military units throughout Europe. I had good friends at every location, and I wanted them to know what was going on and why I wouldn't be at work. He said it would be taken care of and thanked me for being so open with everyone about what was going on and how I was feeling.

The email was sent out that afternoon, and I immediately started getting emails. They were amazing, and most made me cry. I decided to print them out and keep them to read later when I needed a reminder that I was loved or needed a reminder to fight this disease. Everyone was so wonderful and I felt so loved and cared for. I bought a scrapbook and put all the cards, emails, and notes I received in it. It was my "cancer journal," and I wanted to have it so that in the event I died, Brittany would know how everyone cared for her mother. I still have the book to this day.

I went home from work on Tuesday afternoon, and when I turned the corner on the last flight of stairs, I stopped in my tracks. There, on the landing outside my door, were six huge bouquets of colorful flowers. They were beautiful and filled the stairwell with a sweet aroma. I was picking them up when my neighbor across the hallway opened her door.

She smiled at me and asked jokingly, "Who died?" She went on to say that she had four more bouquets in her house because they ran out of room on my landing.

I chuckled and said, "Nobody died. I was diagnosed with cancer on Monday."

I thought she was going to throw herself over the railing. She stammered over her words, and I told her not to worry about it. "It's okay," I said. "I'm not mad, and I know you were only joking with me."

She kept apologizing and asked if there was anything she could do to make it up to me. "Yes," I said.

"Anything, Kim, I'll do anything," she replied.

"Great. Get me some vases and help me get these flowers in them." I shoved a bouquet toward her with a smile, and we walked inside my apartment.

On Wednesday, Dr. Crawford called as promised and asked what I had decided to do. *Not have it* was my first thought, but I knew that wouldn't fly. I told him I had decided to have a mastectomy, followed by immediate reconstruction with a saline implant.

"Are you sure?" he asked me.

"Yes. Now please hang up before I change my mind."

Click. The line went dead. *Bastard*, I thought, but I knew if I would have talked to him anymore I would have second-guessed my decision.

During lunch the next day, I walked over to a bookstore near my office and purchased a book on cancer. I don't remember the name of it, but it was about a woman's battle with breast cancer. It scared the hell out of me. It was full of medical jargon and talked a lot about chemotherapy. The one thing that stuck in my head from that book was the name of the chemotherapy drug: Adriamycin.

The author talked about how pretty this drug is because it has a beautiful, bright red color and looks just like Cherry Kool-Aid. However, the effects can be devastating. The statement that jumped out at me was, "It's not if you lose your hair; it's when you lose your hair." I threw the book away.

The week went on and I grew more nervous with each passing day. It got harder and harder to concentrate on work, and honestly, I didn't do much that week. My key thing was to turn over projects I was working on because I wasn't sure when I would be back.

Friday was the most difficult day for me. I had two hard tasks to accomplish that day. The first was my pre-op at the hospital. I had blood drawn, X-rays taken, an EKG performed, and most important, a talk with Dr. Crawford and the anesthesiologist. Dr. Crawford asked me if I had talked to Brittany about the risks of surgery and the fact that I had a fifty-fifty chance of not coming out of it.

What? First I had to tell my daughter I had cancer, and now I had to tell her I may not come out of surgery alive. There was no way I could do that to her. However, I wanted to prepare her for the worst, just in case. I promised him I would tell her no matter how difficult it would be. He started talking to me some more about the subject, and I asked him to stop. I didn't want to talk about it anymore. "I'll talk to her. Enough said."

When I got back to work, I felt as if I were saying good-bye for good. I cried most of the day and felt as useless as a mashed potato sandwich. I was having a hard time, but my friend George was taking it harder than I was. He barely spoke to me that day and couldn't look at me.

Toward the end of the day, as I was clearing my desk, he asked me if he could walk me to my car. "Of course you can. I wouldn't have it any other way," I told him. I finished saying my good-byes and we walked to the car. As we were walking, I asked him if he would come visit me in the hospital, but he said no.

I was hurt. One of my best friends wasn't going to come see me. I asked him why and he said he couldn't stand to see me like that. He would call me, but that was it. He didn't want to see me hurting and in pain.

I couldn't look him in the eye as he was talking because I didn't want him to see the tears welling up in my eyes. I turned to look at him, and George pulled me into his arms and gave me a hug. I needed that from him. I let myself break down and sob in his arms. "I'm so scared, George. I'm so afraid I'm going to die and Brittany won't have a mom. I don't want to die."

All he said was, "You'll be okay, Little Girl." He pulled away, got into his car, and drove off.

The weekend was pure hell. I was told I would be in the hospital for at least four days, so I made arrangements to have a friend of mine stay at my place while I was in the hospital. I didn't want to disrupt Brittany's life anymore than I had to. I packed a gym bag with some comfortable clothes, toiletries, reading material, and a picture of Brittany.

Sunday morning my sister, her husband, Brittany, and I went to church. The pastor asked if there were any special prayer requests, and I stood up and asked to be remembered in prayer because I was having surgery in the morning for cancer. After that, I was so emotional I could hardly sit in my seat.

After church we all went to lunch. I could barely eat, and the conversation was almost non-existent. My sister kept encouraging me to eat and then to have dessert. I felt as if I were being fattened up for slaughter—like it was my last meal. I was hungry and wanted to eat, but every bite became harder and harder to swallow. I gave up.

We went home, and I let Brittany go out and spend some time with her friends. I called my sister Lori and my brother, Roger, and talked to them. Again, it felt like I was saying good-bye for the last time. I told them that Vickie was going to be at the hospital during the surgery and I would have her call them as soon as she knew something. I said, "I love you," repeatedly and then hung up.

Later that evening, after Brittany had her shower, we went into my bedroom and sat on my bed. She didn't want to talk, but I told her she didn't have a choice because we had to have this conversation. She looked at me and knew instantly I was worried about what I was about to say. For the first time since I told her I had cancer, she seemed like she cared. That made me cry.

I told her about the surgery and what they were going to do. I told her that my friend Lucy was coming to stay with her while I was in the hospital. She liked Lucy, so that was okay with her. I asked her if she would visit me in the hospital, but she said no. She said she didn't like hospitals and didn't want to see me in one. Again, I was hurt, but I understood where she was coming from.

She still knew something was up because she said, "Mommy, what's wrong?" I told her that the surgery I was going to have was very dangerous because it would be long and because they were working close to my heart and lungs. I told her the doctors were going to do their best, but I might not come home from the surgery.

"Does that mean you could die?" she asked.

"Yes, baby girl, it does."

She broke down and said, "Mommy, I don't want you to die. Who would I live with? I don't want to live with my daddy. Mommy, please don't die."

I took her into my arms and told her that I didn't want to, and I hoped to come home to her. She let me hold her for a few minutes, but then pulled away. She dried her tears and told me she was tired and wanted to go to bed. She climbed down off my bed and disappeared. No kiss. No hug. No, "I love you, Mom." Her door slammed shut.

I started crying but stopped when I stood in front of the mirror. Damn you, cancer. Damn you for putting me through this. Damn you for making me feel this way. Damn you for turning my daughter against me. Damn you for making me question my faith and my own strength. Damn you for invading my breast.

I removed my shirt and bra and looked at myself in the mirror. I looked at my breast for a few minutes from every angle. I touched it. I ran my hand over my breast and across my nipple. I wondered what it would look like tomorrow, because tomorrow it would all be gone. Tomorrow I would lose my left breast to cancer.

Chapter 9

Surgery

My surgery was scheduled for 9:00 AM, but I had to be at the hospital at 7:00 to get all of the final screenings done before my surgery. It was early, but early doesn't matter when you don't sleep. And I didn't, at least not much. At that point, time was irrelevant. I didn't need the sleep anyway because I knew I'd be doing enough of it during surgery.

I got up and took a long, hot shower. It would be the last one I got for about a week, so I wanted to soak up every moment of it. I rinsed off and then washed with a special medicated antibacterial soap the hospital gave me.

When I got out of the shower, Brittany was up and getting dressed for school. I went into her room to say good morning, but she wouldn't even look at me. I left and ran to the bathroom to throw up; my nerves had made me sick to my stomach. I put on a pair of sweats and a t-shirt. I felt no need to get all dressed up.

Vickie rang the doorbell and came in to make sure I had everything I needed. I asked her to come into my room for a minute, and I asked Brittany to join us. With tears in my eyes, I looked at Vickie. "What I'm about to ask you is not going to be easy. I need you to promise me something. I need you to promise me that if I don't make it through surgery, you'll fight for custody of Brittany no matter what it takes. Promise me right here and right now in front of Brittany."

If something happened to me, I didn't want Brittany to have to live with her dad for a couple reasons. First, they hardly knew each other. We divorced when she was four, and they were never really close. Second, he was at that time living a lifestyle I didn't approve of, nor one that I wanted her exposed to.

By now we were all crying. Vickie said she would fight for her no matter what. I made her promise me and Brittany right there that she would do it. I also made her sign a note that said the same thing. I had written it during the night when everything was going through my mind. It was about time to go, but I had to do one last thing before we left the house—throw up again.

Vickie grabbed my small suitcase, and I told Hannah good-bye. I picked her up and hugged her and told her to be good for Brittany. I walked around the house, making sure everything was okay for my friend Lucy, who would be staying at the house with Brittany while I was in the hospital.

Vickie looked at the clock and then at me, signaling it was time to go. I put on my jacket and told Brittany I had to go. I grabbed her and hugged her close to me. Tears were running down my cheeks because I was sad and scared to death.

I was sad because Brittany was showing no emotion at all. She hugged me like she was being forced to hug someone she barely knew. Damn it! I needed a hug from her, a real hug from my baby girl. She began to soften up and relax during the hug until she saw me crying. Then she stiffened up and let go.

I was scared because this might be the last time I would see my beautiful baby girl. It might be the last time I held her or smelled the scent of her hair. It might be the last time I heard her voice and her laughter or feel the soft touch of her hand on mine. I hated this.

"Vickie, let's go," I said. "I have to get out of here now." I took one last look at Brittany and closed the door. "I hate you, cancer," I mumbled to myself.

We arrived at the hospital, and since it was so early, we found a good place to park, right by the door. We walked into the hospital, which was eerily quiet, and made our way to the surgery department. We were almost there when I turned to Vickie and told her I needed to make one last stop—to the bathroom, to throw up again. My nerves were getting the best of me.

After my side trip to the bathroom, we made it to the surgery ward, and I got checked in right away. I was given a room where I could change into the appropriate hospital attire and wait. The doctors, nurses, and anesthesiologist would prep me in this room and then take me to the operating room. The room was really bare. It had a bed, a chair, and a television. I had started to calm down a little, but I was still anxious. I was freezing and my whole body was shaking. This happens when I get nervous.

The nurse came in to do the standard stuff: blood pressure, temperature, hospital identification bracelets, and paperwork—lots of paperwork. She asked me when was the last time I had something to eat or drink, verified all the information, and said the doctors and anesthesiologist would be in shortly.

A few minutes later, Dr. Crawford and the plastic surgeon came into the room. As soon as I saw them, I started crying because I knew it was getting close to the time of my surgery and to the time of losing my breast and possibly my life. Dr. Crawford asked if everything was okay, and Vickie told him it had been a rough morning and that I was just really nervous. He squeezed my arm as if to say that everything was going to be alright.

About that time, the anesthesiologist came in to start my IV. She said they would get the IV started and then give me something to calm me down—"a morning glass of wine," she called it.

I'm a difficult stick when it comes to needles and IVs. Not that I'm afraid of them; my veins are. They like to play hide-and-seek with the needles, and when they're caught, they normally explode with a bright blue and black color that stays around for about a week later to taunt me. This time was no different. The anesthesiologist ended up sticking me about three times, with no luck. Part of the problem was that I was shaking uncontrollably because I was so nervous and I couldn't hold my arm steady enough for her to get a good vein.

On the fourth attempt, she was able to get a small IV started. It wouldn't hold up for the surgery, but it would hold up long enough to give me drugs. I needed the drugs because I was shaking so bad I swore the bed jiggled around the room a little. After she capped off the

IV, she left to get my medicine. My head was still buried in my sister's arms, and I was crying.

The anesthesiologist came back to the room with a needle full of something. She said it wouldn't put me to sleep, but I wouldn't remember anything from this point forward. She put the tip of the needle into the IV access, but I asked her to stop. Everybody stopped and looked at me, as if they were in shock.

I looked over at Vickie and asked her to repeat the promise she made to me earlier. "I promise that if something happens to you during surgery, I'll fight for custody of Brittany," she said.

"Thank you," I whispered. I looked over at my doctors, who looked away because they, too, had tears in their eyes.

I nodded to the anesthesiologist to go ahead with the injection. She started pushing the medicine into the IV in my hand. I immediately started feeling a little woozy and looked over at Vickie one last time. "I love you, Sis. Tell Brittany that I love her very much." That was the last thing I said that I remember.

I thought I went to sleep right after that, but Vickie told me later I was wide awake. She said I was sitting in bed and talking as if everything was normal. I talked to the doctors and carried on real conversations. It's so weird that I don't remember any of it.

The next thing I remember was being really cold. I wasn't sure of anything else, but I also thought I heard voices and people talking. I also heard a faint beeping sound that soon began to fade, along with everything else. When I woke up, I was in a bed. A set of white curtains surrounded me on all sides. I was covered up but wasn't aware of any IVs, tubing, or machines. The only other thing I saw was a bright light above my bed.

About the time I got focused on the light, a man leaned over my bed. His head was dead center in the bright light above, so it looked as if he had a halo. He had the most beautiful blue eyes I've ever seen in my life. Everything was peaceful and beautiful. Then it hit me.

I'm dead. Oh, my God, I'm dead. I didn't make it out of surgery. Brittany is going to grow up without her mom. My sister must be devastated. Oh, no, she has to tell Brittany and the rest of the family I died. Will she be able to do it? What will my friends at work do? What will Brittany do? I must have been thinking these things out loud because that same man leaned over my bed and asked me if I had said something.

"Are you my angel?" I asked him.

"I don't know about being your angel, but I'm your nurse."

"I'm not dead?"

"No, sweetie, you're not dead. You're in the recovery room. You just had surgery for breast cancer."

"Cool I'm alive," I said before returning to never-never land.

My next recollection was when I was wheeled down the hallway to my room. I could hear my sister talking to someone. I remember saying, "Hey, Sis, I'm alive," before I was out again.

I heard voices when I was waking up again. This time Vickie was talking to a friend of mine who had stopped by to check on me. It seemed like it had been hours, but it must have been only a few minutes because I wasn't in my room yet. I was still being wheeled down the hallway.

Vickie and my friend were talking about how the surgery went and how painful the recovery would be for me later. They were talking about the final cancer diagnosis, and I remember Vickie saying it would be a few days before we would know anything specific.

They continued to talk about me like I wasn't even there, so I began to smile. Vickie said, "Look at that smile on her face. She must be having a good dream." I smiled bigger because they had no idea I could hear and understand every word they were saying. I just couldn't open my eyes, and I couldn't get any words out.

Once in my room, the orderlies woke me up to tell me I had to move over into my real bed. I immediately tried to push myself up with my arms, but searing pain shot through both sides of my chest. I started crying and said I couldn't do it. They tried to help me, but it just hurt more.

There was only one way to do this, and it's the same way a Band-Aid needs to be taken off—just rip it off and get it over with. I took a deep breath, dug my elbows into the bed, and forced myself up and over onto the other bed. Using this same technique, I was able to get myself to the head of the bed and in a resting position. Within seconds, I had passed out from the pain.

When I woke up again it was around 6:00 PM. I was given some food, and I was surprised to find it wasn't Jell-O or chicken broth. It was real food, and I could eat some of it. I was still groggy from surgery, so I wasn't 100 percent sure of my surroundings. I do remember a couple of people from my work there, but nothing else.

My visitors didn't stay long, and I asked the nurse if I could go to the bathroom. She brought me a bed pan and placed it under my butt. Peeing while lying down on a plastic bucket is not easy. Having my sister and medical staff standing just outside the curtain listening for the sound of trickling urine made it more difficult. Stage fright set in, and I couldn't go.

The nurse came in and said she had a portable potty she could bring in for me, the kind where the bed pan is built into the seat of the chair. I said that would be fine because I really had to go. She brought in the portable chair and helped me out of bed and onto the potty. Ah, instant relief. I swear I went to the bathroom for ten minutes. When I was done going to the bathroom, the nurse handed me some toilet paper. I reached down and tried to wipe myself, but I couldn't. The pain was so intense I almost passed out. I started sobbing and said I couldn't do it. The nurse took the toilet paper and said she would do it for me. "You don't have to do that," I said. She said it was okay because it's part of her job.

I was humiliated, embarrassed, and mad. I couldn't believe I was thirty-five years old and had to have someone wipe me. *I hate you, cancer. I hate what you've turned me into.*

After I finished, the nurse told me that Dr. Crawford said I had to sit in a chair for at least fifteen minutes. I never realized sitting in a chair could be so tiring and so painful. After about five minutes I started getting really nauseous. The nurse gave me a shot of something to keep me from throwing up and helped me get back into bed, even though the doctor wanted me to sit for a while. She said she would let me try it again later after I had rested a little longer.

A few minutes later a different nurse came in and said I was moving to a new room. I started crying because I didn't want to go through the pain of moving beds again. She said they would move my bed, too, so I wouldn't have to physically move. I was fine with that.

Remember when I said that having Vickie as my sister had its perks? This was one of those times; I got a private room with my own bathroom and a window. It was a small room, but it was private, and I didn't have to share my television, shower, or toilet.

Once I got settled into my new room, the nurses came in and

hooked up my self-medicating pain pump with morphine. I was in so much pain from the incisions that I needed some instant relief. I immediately hit the button, and it was "Good night, Irene."

When I woke up again it was late. I wasn't sure of the time, but it was dark outside. I was more coherent this time and could take stock of my surroundings. I was alone, but I could hear my sister talking. She was outside my room on her cell phone, and she was talking quietly. She was saying something about more tests and that Dr. Crawford was a little worried about something.

I started getting mad. She was talking about me like I wasn't there. I called her name and she walked into the room. "Hi, honey, I didn't know you were awake," she said. I asked her what she was talking about. She said it was nothing.

"Don't lie to me. I heard you saying something about the doctor being worried and something about more tests."

She looked surprised and said Dr. Crawford had talked to her about my Pap smear results. They were worried because it had come back showing atypical cells, and given the fact that I was just diagnosed with breast cancer, it might be a cause for concern.

I said I wasn't worried about that right now. "I just want to talk to my daughter," I said. Vickie said it was late and not to worry because she had called Brittany to tell her I was out of surgery and that things went fine.

"I don't care. I want to talk to her right now," I said. She dialed my home phone and told Brittany that I wanted to talk to her. She handed me the phone, and it was like hearing the angels sing.

"Hi, Mommy, are you okay?"

"I am now, baby girl. I'm a little sore, but you've made it all better. I miss you so much, and I can't wait to see you. Are you doing okay?"

"Yes, Mommy, I'm fine. I was worried about you."

"No need to worry now, baby girl. I'm fine and will be home soon."

"Mommy, can I come see you?"

This was something I had been waiting to hear, and tears began rolling down my face. "Of course you can come to see me, baby girl. It would mean the world to me."

Brittany said she would come to see me in a few days and then said, "Good night, Mommy. I love you so much."

"I love you, too, baby girl. I love you too."

I figured I could have slept without pain meds that night because I was so happy. I told Vickie it was okay for her to leave because I was really tired and she needed to get some rest too. She was heading out at 4:00 AM to visit the troops in Afghanistan for Christmas, and I wanted her to get her rest. She didn't want to leave because she didn't want me to be alone, especially since she would be gone for the next few days.

"I'll be fine, Vickie. Besides, I'm going to be in the hospital three to four days, and that won't be much fun for you. I'll also have friends stopping by to keep me company."

She finally agreed to go on her trip, but I asked her if she would at least stay with me until I fell asleep. She said yes. I remember her sitting on the side of my bed. The last thing I remember was her kissing me on the forehead and saying, "I love you, Sis."

As it turned out, the night was kind of restless due to the pain. The only sleep I got was aided by morphine. Every four hours, a nurse wheeled in the noisiest blood pressure machine to check my vitals. She also had to check my bandages and empty my drains. I had two on each side of my chest to drain off the excess fluid and blood that collected around the surgery site.

As if the noisy blood pressure machine wasn't enough, she would turn on the light directly above my head. The ironic thing is the doctors and nurses were always telling me to get some rest. Well, I was trying to.

Other than the vital checks every four hours, I was having severe hallucinations from the morphine. I thought I was dreaming at first, until I realized I was wide awake and talking to the nurses when it happened. The hallucination first occurred as an enormous pink bunny with three eyes. It wouldn't say anything. It would just sit above my door on the frame and point at me, but its hands were where his feet should be and vice versa. I kept trying to get the nurse to watch him, but she said there was nothing there. What was wrong with her? He was right there above my door ready to pounce on her. How could she not see him?

In addition to the rabbit, I saw bugs, machines, monsters, and other giants. I heard people talking to me and other weird noises. I was so afraid of what I would see or hear that I stopped self-medicating.

I begged for them to take the morphine pump away because I

don't like taking pain medicine and because I didn't want any more hallucinations. One day was enough, and I needed to be able to function without pain meds. They finally agreed and stopped the morphine, taking the machine—and the monsters—away.

The day after my surgery was filled with visitors, flowers, and phone calls. It made me feel so good to know I was cared about and loved. I didn't get out of bed much that day, other than to go to the bathroom and sit up to eat. Later that night Dr. Crawford came in and said he wanted me to get up and walk the hallway.

Begrudgingly, I did it. It was painful at first, but it made me feel better. The walk kept my muscles from getting weak and kept me moving. It also helped get my internal plumbing working again.

My second night in the hospital was better. A nurse still woke me up every few hours, but I slept better in those four hours with only the help of Tylenol 3 with codeine. When I woke up the next morning, I was told I could take a shower. *Thank you, God.* It had to be quick, and my drains had to be taped up, but it was better than a sponge bath again. After my shower, I decided to take a walk. As I walked up and down the hall, it was amazing how many people were there alone and had nobody visiting them, even though it was close to Christmas. One woman in particular got my attention.

She was older and also in a private room. As I would walk past her room, she would turn to me. Her face was expressionless, and her room was dark. She had a television and a window, but the television was always off and the shades were always drawn. I couldn't believe that nobody was there to visit her.

When I got back to my room, I was exhausted. Dr. Crawford was there waiting for me. He said it was nice to see me up and walking. I sat down in the chair, and he said he wanted to talk to me about my test results. *Uh-oh.* I wasn't sure I was ready for more bad news from him.

He said my tumor was 2.3 cm in size and the margins were clear. The bad thing was that it had already spread to my lymph nodes. They had taken out nineteen lymph nodes, and the cancer was in two of nineteen. Due to the size of the tumor and the lymph node involvement, I was classified in Stage 2B. The stages range from 0 to 4. A Stage 4 diagnosis is considered terminal. I was smack dead in the middle, and my cancer finally was given a name: Invasive Ductal Carcinoma.

I was really upset because there was lymph node involvement, not what I was hoping for. We talked a little more, and he said that based on the diagnosis and the lymph node involvement, I would certainly need chemotherapy. He would speak with the hospital oncologist to see if I would need radiation also.

> *Invasive Ductal Carcinoma is a common form of breast cancer that breaks out of the milk ducts and invades surrounding tissue. It has the potential to spread into lymph and blood systems.*

Dr. Crawford said he would let me get some rest and got ready to leave. Before he left my room, he helped me get back into bed and get settled. He sat down on the side of my bed and took my hand. "Kim, now is a good time to take stock of your life and always take time to stop and smell the roses." I nodded in agreement. He was almost to the door when he turned and said, "If everything goes well tonight, and you're up to it, I'll let you go home tomorrow afternoon." I was so happy. I thanked him and he left.

I turned off the television and took a nap. The walk and the shower exhausted me, so it wasn't hard to sleep. I slept until they brought my lunch tray in. I got out of bed to sit in my chair and eat. Just as I started eating, my phone rang.

I answered it and was surprised to hear the voice of Mr. Parker, an older gentleman I worked with. He was a quiet man who kept to himself and rarely talked to anyone. He said he was thinking of me and wanted to call to see how I was doing. "I'm doing okay," I told him. "I just got some more bad news this morning. My labs came back, and the cancer has spread to my lymph nodes. It was in two of nineteen."

Then he said something that made me feel better, something I still remember to this day: "At least it wasn't in nineteen out of nineteen. You just got great news, if you ask me." He was right. I was looking at the glass half-empty instead of half-full. I thanked him for calling and hung up.

After lunch I took another walk. This time I could walk about twenty minutes before tiring. The older woman was still alone, but this time she smiled at me when I walked by. The last trip by I waved at her, and she nodded in acknowledgement.

I spent the afternoon reading a book a dear friend had given me,

Love, Medicine and Miracles, by Bernie Siegel. It was about how the human spirit and attitude can heal. This is an amazing book, and I recommend it to anyone who is facing cancer or a life-threatening illness.

When the orderlies brought in my dinner, I went to wash up before I ate. When I came out of the bathroom, I was surprised to find George standing in the doorway. "Hello, Little Girl," he said. I couldn't believe he came to see me! I began crying because it meant the world to me to have him there. George said he wasn't going to stay because he didn't want to see me like this. He came over, kissed me on the forehead, gave me a card, and walked out the door.

I ate dinner and then had the best visitor in the whole wide world—Brittany. Lucy had brought her up to see me. Brittany came in and gave me the biggest hug. It hurt, but I wouldn't let her see the pain on my face. "I miss you, Mommy," she said. "When can you come home?"

"Well, baby girl, the doctor said that if I'm doing well and I feel up to it, he might let me come home tomorrow." A big smile spread across her face, and she said that would be great. We spent the evening watching television and taking walks. We had a snack together, and then the nurses came in to check my bandages, take my vitals, and empty my drains. I asked them if they could come back and do it after Brittany left, and they agreed.

I told Brittany she should probably go home because it was getting late and she had to get up early to go to school. She didn't want to leave, but I told her if all went well, I would be home tomorrow when she got home from school. She hugged me tight and told me she loved me so much. I said, "Ditto, baby girl."

Brittany and Lucy left, and after the nurses checked my vitals one more time, I was out for the night. The doctor had told the nurses I didn't have to have my vitals checked until the morning shift, so I could sleep through the night for the first time since my surgery. What a difference it made being able to sleep the entire night without being woken up every four hours.

On Thursday morning I was up before breakfast was brought in. After breakfast, the nurses came in for vitals and removed my drains. That was fun. When they pulled out the drains, it felt like they were pulling snakes out of my body. The tubes for the drains were about ten inches long and coiled inside my body. I felt like I was free for the first time since entering the hospital. I had no IVs and no drains. The large bandages were gone, and only Band-Aids were covering the stitches.

I took a long shower, and when I came out, Dr. Crawford was there. *Uh-oh*, I thought to myself, *more bad news.* Instead, he was there to tell me I could go home after more blood work was done to make sure I had no sign of infection. I should be out of there by noon.

The nurse came in, checked my vitals, and took some blood for the tests. She was sure they wouldn't find anything, so they went ahead and let me get dressed and call my friend for a ride. I looked around my room, which was full of flowers, balloons, and cards.

A beautiful bouquet of roses had just been delivered to me that morning, and we had to set them in the bathroom because I had nowhere else in the room for them. The nurse asked me if I was going to take them all home, and I said no because I already had a lot there too.

She said it was okay, that they would throw them away. I said, "No, give them to other people on the floor who don't have any." She said that was a lovely idea, and she would take care of it. I let her know I would take care of the bouquet of roses that I just received. I wanted to give them to the older woman at the end of the hall who was always alone, but I wanted to do it myself.

I took the roses and walked down to her room. I knocked on her door, and she turned to me and smiled. I asked her if I could come in, and her face lit up. "Yes," she said weakly.

I told her that I was leaving the hospital and I wanted her to have these beautiful flowers. I set them on her window sill, and she couldn't take her eyes off them. I sat down on the side of her bed, and tears welled up in her eyes as she took hold of my hand. "Thank you for the flowers," she said.

"You're welcome." I sat there with her for a few minutes.

"So you're going home today?" she asked. "Why were you in the hospital?"

I told her about my cancer and that I had a long road ahead of me for recovery. We talked a little about Christmas and other things, but I could tell it tired her to talk. I asked her when she was going to get to go home. What she said still brings tears to my eyes when I think about her.

"Honey, I won't be going home. When I leave here, it'll be in a hearse. My heart is bad, and I'm waiting on a transplant. I know it'll never happen, so I'm ready to go."

I was speechless, which is unusual for me. I sat there looking at her as she patted my hand, as if to say it would be all right. All I could do was wish her well and give her a hug.

I knew she was tired, so I told her I'd let her get her rest. I turned to look at her before I left, but she had already turned her eyes to the wall. I went back to see her a week later when I was at the hospital getting a checkup, but her room was dark and the bed was empty. I didn't ask. I didn't want to know.

I went back to my room that day and waited on my walking papers from Dr. Crawford. He came in around lunch and officially discharged me. He went over my home care instructions: no lifting, no strenuous activity, lots of rest, and lots of laughter. No problem there! He told me to keep a positive attitude no matter what happens on my road to recovery, and it would be a much easier one.

He hugged me and thanked me for making his job easier. He said that I was an ideal patient with the right attitude and demeanor for a quick recovery. I was given my list of follow-up appointments with him and my plastic surgeon. I also got a new one, my initial meeting with the oncology department. That was a mood-changer.

The drive home from the hospital was amazing. I noticed things I hadn't noticed before. The snow was beautiful, and there was lots of it. It was cold and damp, but to me, it was perfect for two reasons. First, I had been in a hospital bed for four days with no connection to the outside world except for what I could see through my tiny window. Second, and most important, I was alive and had a whole new outlook on life.

When I got home, Lucy helped me upstairs and asked me if I wanted her to stay for a little while. "No," I said. "I need to rest, and I want Brittany all to myself when she gets home." I thanked her for everything she had done for me and Brittany, and she left.

Hannah was so happy to see me that she wouldn't leave me alone. I went against the doctor's orders and took her out for a walk. It was nice to get out. I took her onto the tennis courts right in front of my building and let her run. I'm not sure who enjoyed the outing more—Hannah or me.

When Brittany got home, she was so excited to see me. That night was magical because we just lay on the couch and snuggled. When it was time for bed, we reversed roles, and she tucked me in. I couldn't sleep in my bed due to the pain when lying flat, so she helped me into my La-Z-Boy recliner, which became my temporary bed. Then, for the first time in almost three weeks, I got a kiss and a real goodnight hug from my baby girl.

The night was restless for me because I wasn't used to being at home. I ended up taking some pain medication just so I could sleep. I got up the next morning and fixed Brittany some breakfast before she went to school. On her way out the door, I looked at her school calendar and realized it was Friday, December 21, the night of my office Christmas party.

Vickie had gotten home from her trip to Afghanistan late Thursday night, so I called her and asked her if she would take me to my Christmas party. She said I shouldn't go out, but I told her I really didn't want to miss it and that it would mean so much to me. After a few more minutes of discussion, she agreed to take me.

Around 4:30 PM it started snowing, and it quickly turned into blizzard-like conditions. I called my office to see if they were still having the party, and they said yes. By the time Vickie got home, it was nearing 6:30 and we had almost five inches of snow on the ground. Once again she tried to talk me out of it. I told her I was going to that party even if it meant I had to walk. She drove.

We got to the party just as everyone was sitting down for dinner. We walked in, and you could have heard a pin drop. Everyone gasped when they saw me, and then immediately stood up and started clapping. Cue the tears. People started coming up to hug me, but Vickie acted as my bodyguard. She knew I was still extremely sore from my surgery and was afraid they would squeeze me a little too hard.

We sat down at a table with my commander and his family and some other co-workers. The commander got up to speak before the dinner started. He was talking about how 2001 had been a tough year. He said that since the terrorist attacks of September 11 had happened, we should all realize that things can happen very quickly and change our world forever. He went on to say that we have to stay focused and vigilant and find a little courage and motivation to get us back on track. Then he said that if he ever needed some inspiration, courage, or motivation to get him through a difficult time, he would just look at me.

He said I had been through so much already, and that I still had a long way to go. Then he turned to me and said, "Kim, I admire you and everything you've been through and are about to go through. You're certainly an inspiration to me and so many others. I'm glad you're here with us tonight."

Everyone stood up and started clapping again. I reached for the tissues.

Chapter 10

The Road to Chemo

I would be starting chemotherapy soon, so Dr. Crawford said I should get a few other things out of the way before it started. He told me to make sure my immunizations were up-to-date and get any dental work done beforehand. They didn't want me doing something that could weaken my immune system during treatment.

Around January 6, 2002, I went to the dental clinic for my cleaning. As I was standing in line to be checked in, I turned around and was shocked to see my family doctor standing in line a few people behind me. After we both got checked in, I went up and talked to him.

"Doc, do you remember when I came to see you in January due to a lump in my breast?"

He had a curious look on his face and said, "It's January now."

"Last January. I came in with pain in my left breast and told you I had found a lump."

"Yes, I vaguely remember. What did I do about it?"

"Absolutely nothing," I replied. "You told me it was nothing to worry about, and it was probably nothing more than a cyst. Well, unfortunately for me this cyst was cancer, and now I have a saline implant where my left breast used to be."

He was speechless at first. Then he said, "Yes, I heard about that. I'm so sorry. Is there anything I can do for you?"

"No, not for me," I said. "There's nothing you can do to bring my left breast back or change the fact that I have cancer. What you can do for me is to promise to listen to your patients from this point on and take them seriously. Don't blow them off because you think it's nothing."

He agreed and said if there was anything Brittany or I needed to call him directly instead of going through the appointment center. "I mean it," he said. "If you need medicine or refills or Brittany needs an appointment, call me directly." He then handed me a business card with his direct number on it and walked away with a look on his face that I'll never forget. I think that's what guilt and remorse look like.

The next week brought my first in a series of appointments with the oncology department. I was extremely nervous, but I knew I wouldn't be taking any treatments at my first appointment. I was nervous at the prospect of finding out what was to come. I was told to expect to be there about three to four hours because I had chemo orientation, and then I would meet with the doctor.

I showed up in the oncology department and was met by Rebecca, the most pleasant nurse I've ever met. She was so nice and upbeat, and she made me very comfortable. My first order of business was to get a tour of the oncology department.

I was shown the main room and the private rooms. The main room was large and open with lots of chairs that look like La-Z-Boy recliners. There were televisions, magazines, movies, books, and some games to help patients pass the time, because one chemo session can take anywhere from three to six hours. The private rooms were for the really sick patients who were considered terminal. At least that's what the setup was like at my treatment center.

After my tour I had to watch a video, and then I received lots of information to take home to read. Rebecca and I talked a lot about chemo. She asked me how my veins were, and I said horrible. I told her they were tiny and deep and they roll. She said I would be a good candidate for the port-a-cath. I asked her about it, and she explained it was a catheter that went into my chest just underneath the skin. It would have a small tube that went directly into the main artery and would deliver the drugs directly into my system. I was a little hesitant until she told me about the problems I could have if I didn't get a port-a-cath.

If my vein were to collapse during treatment, it could cause severe chemical burns that could destroy the surrounding veins and tissue. I chose the port. She said she would request one and let the doctor know. We finished the paperwork, and she took me to meet the oncologist. Dr. Figgs was very nice but very busy. He introduced himself and got right to the point.

"Your cancer is very aggressive," he said.

Well, its freaking nice to meet you too, I thought to myself.

"The cancer has already spread to your lymph nodes, as you already know, but what you don't know is that it's also estrogen positive. This means that the estrogen your body is producing is what was feeding your cancer and making it grow. We don't know yet if it's HER 2 positive, but we'll find that out later. I recommend four cycles of chemotherapy. Your chemo cocktail will consist of Adriamycin and Cytoxan. We'll start your chemotherapy about a week after your surgery to have your port put in. Any questions?"

> *If veins collapse during chemotherapy, it could cause several chemical burns that could destroy the surrounding veins and tissue.*

"Yes, can you start back over at the beginning?" I asked. He looked at me like I was crazy. I told him I was only kidding. I had no questions because I didn't know what to ask.

He called General Surgery and spoke with Dr. Crawford about getting the port implanted. My surgery was set for January 19. He said it would be a small procedure and would take about forty-five minutes. My first chemo treatment was scheduled for January 25.

Dr. Figgs continued to talk about my treatments. He said after chemo, I would have about eight weeks of radiation therapy, and they would send me back to the states for that.

"Stop right there," I said. "You can't send me back to the states. What about my daughter? I'm a single parent. She's in school, and I'm not going to leave her here alone without family or pull her out of school to take her with me."

He said I didn't have a choice, but he would review my case with a few of his colleagues to see if I needed the radiation.

Before I left, Dr. Figgs said I had to have a few more tests done before I started chemo. He ordered a head and chest CT scan, a bone scan, and a MUGA scan. The head and chest CT and the bone scan were to see if the cancer had spread to any of those areas. The MUGA scan (which stands for MUltiple Gated Acquisition) was to check the muscles and valves of the heart. The drug Adriamycin could potentially cause damage to the heart muscles, so they wanted to ensure my heart was healthy before we got started. So, the cure for my cancer was so powerful it could destroy other parts of my body. Unbelievable.

The surgery for the port implant went smoothly, but was very painful. I had the CT scans done of my head and chest, both of which were clean and showed no signs of cancer. I did have a few spots on my lungs, and now some on my liver that doctors continue to watch to this day.

Next was my bone scan. When I showed up for that, I was injected with some contrast and was taken to the exam room. They helped me up on the table and asked me to lie down. I was still very sore from the surgery, and I winced a little as I lay back. The technician asked me if I had fallen on the ice, and I told him that I had just had a mastectomy and a port implant and that I was a little sore. He was standing right beside me and stopped what he was doing. He looked at me and asked, "Do you have a prosthetic device in your bra?"

"Does it matter?" I asked him.

"Yes, because the prosthetic device has to be taken out before the scan. We won't be able to scan through it."

"Oh, I see." Without hesitation, I reached my hand into my shirt, and as I was pulling out my hand I said, "Okay, can you hold this for me, please?"

He had a shocked look on his face and was stammering. He was trying to say something. His face was bright red, so I decided to let him off the hook. "I'm just messing with you, man," I said. "I don't have a prosthetic device, but I do have an implant, and I'm afraid I can't remove it."

"That's fine," he said and started the exam.

I bet he had fun explaining to the other technicians why his face was so red. I know I shouldn't have messed with him, but it was so easy and it made the test a little more fun.

I was really worried about my bone scan because a woman I had worked with in the past was battling bone cancer that started out as breast cancer. Unfortunately, two days after I had my bone scan, she lost her battle, leaving behind a husband, a four-year-old daughter, and a nine-month-old son.

When I heard the news, I immediately picked up the phone and called Dr. Figgs for my results. He said the test was back, but he hadn't read it yet.

"I'll hold," I told him.

"But, Kim I have a patient and I—"

"I'll hold."

Knowing how stubborn I was, he knew I wouldn't give up, so he asked me to hold on. "Kim, your test is clean. There's no sign of cancer in your bones."

"Thank you, Doc, but more important, thank you, God." I apologized for my behavior and attitude and thanked him once again for giving me my results. With the bone and MUGA scans clean, there was nothing to stop me from starting my first round of chemotherapy. Yippee.

Chapter 11

Chemotherapy

Chemotherapy is almost always a necessary evil when treating cancer. It is only in rare cases when a person does not have to have chemotherapy in order to treat this disease. It also varies from patient to patient. Some will need more treatments, while others will need only a few. Some patients will have chemotherapy before surgery and then continue the treatments after they have recovered. Some will have two or more different types of medicine and receive them intravenously, while others will have only one type and take it orally.

The side effects also vary from person to person. They can range from severe, where a person experiences every possible side effect, to mild, where a person experiences only one or two of the most common side effects.

This chapter is about my experience with chemotherapy. I have broken it down by each treatment so it will be easier to understand the full cycle of treatments, how each one affected me, and how I dealt with them.

Treatment #1

January 25, 2002, was my first chemotherapy treatment. I was nervous but excited in a way. I didn't know what to expect with the chemo and the side effects, but I knew I was ready to start the drugs that were going to kill all the bad cells in my body. Unfortunately, they were going to kill good cells too.

Vickie and I showed up in the oncology department and I was checked in. My blood was drawn so the staff could get a starting blood count. After the counts came back good, the call was placed to the pharmacy to prepare my chemo cocktail. I was taken into the chemotherapy room. I was the first one there.

I sat down in a large, comfortable chair while Vickie pulled up a chair right beside me. She was talking to me to take my mind off of what was about to happen, but I had no idea what she was saying. The next thing I knew Rebecca walked in with a large vial of medicine that was bright red— Adriamycin. This drug is so potent that it has to be injected by hand and injected very slowly. Rebecca wore a breathing mask and gloves that went up to her elbows.

Adriamycin is a vesicant that can cause extensive tissue damage and blistering if it leaks from the vein.

"Are you ready?" she asked. I nodded, but thought, *Is anybody ever ready for this?* With my nod, she started pushing on the end of the pump filled with my medicine. I felt like I was watching it in slow motion as the medicine snaked its way through the tubing and into my chest. As soon as it disappeared into my chest, I started getting nauseous and almost threw up.

Vickie and Rebecca must have noticed a change in me, because Vickie squeezed my hand and Rebecca asked me what was wrong. I told her I thought I was going to throw up, and she started laughing. "It's all in your head," she said. "It's all mind over matter." With that she reached over and grabbed a small towel and covered up the tubing so I couldn't see it. Presto, it worked.

As Rebecca was pushing the medicine in, she was telling me more about it. She explained the port and why it was a good idea for me to have it. Adriamycin is a vesicant, a chemical that causes extensive tissue damage and blistering if it leaks from the vein. Since my veins were not the best for continued IV use, Adriamycin could cause me some serious problems. It would also turn my urine red, but she said that I shouldn't worry because the color should go away within a few days. However, if it didn't, I needed to go to the emergency room immediately.

She also told me about the large bottle of pills that she had given me earlier. The pills were my anti-nausea medicine. I was to take four about two hours before each treatment, two just before I started treatment, two more immediately following treatment, and four more three times a day for the first five days after treatment.

After about forty-five minutes, the first part of the treatment was done, so the nurse prepared my second half of the cocktail—Cytoxan. This was to be run through a normal IV, so I was free to get up and walk around the hospital floor. As soon as the Cytoxan started, I told Rebecca that I had to go to the bathroom. She laughed and said I just wanted to see if my urine was red. Of course I did. I've never seen my urine red, and I wanted to see something I'd never seen before.

Rebecca cleared me to leave the area (but I could not leave the floor) while the other chemo drug was infused. She gave me strict instructions about going to the bathroom. I had to use the bathroom in the oncology ward and nowhere else. My sister had to use the one outside the ward because the chemicals in my urine could be harmful to a non-cancer patient. Rebecca also said that when I was at home, since I had only one bathroom, I had to flush three to four times to get all the chemicals out and had to spray Lysol before and after using the bathroom. It was a lot of work but a small price to pay for Brittany's health and well-being.

Before I knew it, my chemo session was over. I took two anti-nausea pills, and we talked a little more about what to expect. Rebecca told me the chemo would take its toll on my immune system starting around day five and come to full impact on day ten. I was told I needed to keep myself quarantined during these five days, and on day ten, I would have to go to the clinic to have blood drawn. If my white blood count dropped to four hundred or less, I would have to be hospitalized immediately. She said I was more likely to die from an infection than from the cancer itself. That scared me.

Another thing I had to be careful of was fresh fruit and vegetables. If I was going to eat them, they had to be cleaned by someone wearing gloves. Then that person would have to change gloves before the food was cooked or given to me to eat. My body couldn't take the risk of infection from any pesticides on the food. It was too much to worry about, so I gave up fresh fruits and vegetables during my treatments. I was also told that I couldn't drink tap water; strictly bottled water for me.

Before we left, Rebecca asked me if I had any questions. I had just one. "How long will it take before I lose my hair?" I asked. She said it happened to most people after their second treatment, but everyone was different.

Vickie and I left the hospital and headed home. About every five minutes, she was asking me if I was okay. I guess she was worried I was going to throw up in her car. I said I was fine, but I was really hungry. No, famished. We drove to a place called Nicks Chicken, the German equivalent to KFC. We got food to take home, but I ate most of mine on the way. When I got home, I also ate a piece of Brittany's chicken and then fixed myself a sandwich. At that point, I think I could have taken a bite out of my kitchen table. My ravenous appetite was caused by the steroids in my anti-nausea medicine. By the end of all my chemo treatments, which was a little more than four months, I had gained nearly seventy pounds.

I took my medicine like I was supposed to before I went to bed. I got up the next morning and went to the office. My commander couldn't believe I was at work. I told him I was fine and that I *needed* to be there. I also told him about my immune system and how it would be weakened for a few days after my chemotherapy session. He said it would be no problem because I could just stay home during that time. I thanked him and told him how much that meant to me.

I couldn't believe how good I was feeling. I swear they gave me a placebo instead of chemo. I felt nothing—no pain, no nausea, no fever, no aches, nothing. These chemo treatments were going to be a piece of cake.

The day before I left work to go home and start my five-day sabbatical, my co-workers called me into the conference room. They asked me to write down a list of my favorite foods that Brittany and I loved. I was not to ask any questions. After I gave them my list of foods, they told me what was going on.

Everyone in the office was signing up to be my buddy for a week at a time. This buddy would be responsible for helping me with whatever

I needed: walking my dog, cleaning my house, doing laundry, driving me to appointments, and taking Brittany anywhere she needed to go. On Sunday, this buddy was responsible for bringing me dinner that would last for a few days so I wouldn't have to cook. They gave me a copy of my buddy list, which was filled in all the way through the end of April (my last chemo treatment). It had all my buddies' phone numbers, so I could contact them whenever I needed them. I was so blessed with so many good friends and co-workers.

On day five I locked myself in my house to protect myself from germs. When Brittany came home from school, I made her change clothes so I could immediately throw them in the washer. I also made her take a shower as soon as she got home, and I wore a mask and gloves to handle her backpack. It sucked and she hated it, but I wanted to live.

February 12 came eighteen days after my first treatment and was turning out to be another ordinary day. When I got to my desk, I removed my military cap and almost passed out. I had just seen a few hairs fall. I reached up, took some hair between my fingers, closed my eyes, and pulled. When I opened my eyes, I held lots of hair between my fingers, and I didn't even feel them come out.

I started crying and pulled a few more strands out with my fingers. I couldn't believe it was coming out so easy and I wasn't feeling it. A co-worker walked by and saw me crying. He asked what was wrong, but I couldn't say anything. Instead, I showed him. He hugged me and said it would be okay. He reminded me that I knew this was supposed to happen, so I shouldn't be too surprised. My commander walked by and wondered what was going on. I showed him too. He started laughing and pointed to his own bald head. "At least yours will grow back," he said. That worked. We all broke out in fits of laughter. He was right. My hair would grow back.

When I went home that night, I went downstairs and asked my neighbor to cut my hair really short. Sandra said she was highlighting someone's hair, but I could come in and wait if I wanted. I went in, and she had just finished putting the bleach on the woman's hair. I walked into the kitchen, where she had her beautician's chair, and started yelling. "How could you do this to me? Don't you know what you're doing? All I wanted was highlights and now my hair is falling out. Look!"

I reached up and pulled out a chunk of hair, and then I turned to look at the mortified woman who was sitting in the chair with a hair full of bleach. I thought she and Sandra were both about to start crying, so I decided to let them know I was only joking. I told the customer that I was going through chemo and my hair was starting to fall out. She was relieved, but she never went back to Sandra to get her hair done. Oops.

After the woman left, I thought Sandra was going to kill me, so I quickly turned the conversation to cutting my hair. She asked me if I was sure I wanted to get my hair cut so short. I explained it was falling out pretty fast, and I figured it would be easier to take with it being shorter. After discussing how to cut it, I told her to just do her best and cut it really short. I almost cried when I saw myself in the mirror, but I had to deal with it. At least having short hair was better than having no hair. That was going to happen sooner rather than later. Looking at my hair in the mirror, I said, "Great, now I'll never get a date for Valentine's Day."

Valentine's Day fell on a Thursday, and I didn't have a date, or so I thought. About 6:00 PM there was a knock at my door. I opened the door to a very handsome man. He was there to take me out to dinner so I wouldn't be alone for Valentine's Day. This handsome man was my brother-in-law. I didn't care that it was a "pity" date because I had fun.

Saturday morning I woke up and noticed a lot of hair on my pillow. I didn't wash it that morning because I was afraid more would fall out. I put some gel in my hair to hold it in place, gave it a spiky appearance, and refused to touch it. I wouldn't touch it, but Brittany sure did.

We were sitting on the couch watching television, and she was commenting about how spiky and stiff my hair looked. I told her it was the only way I could style it since it was falling out so fast. By keeping the gel in it and not washing it, I was hoping it would last a few more days. A few minutes later she was laughing so hard she had tears in her eyes. I turned around to look at her, and she was holding an entire "spike" of my hair. I didn't even feel her pull it out. She wanted to do more, but I told her I didn't want to walk around with tiny bald spots all over my head. I pretended to be upset, but I had to admit later that it was really funny.

On Sunday morning I got up and looked in the mirror. I needed to take a shower because nothing was going to keep me out of church. I started the shower and backed underneath the water because I didn't want to see my hair fall out. It was sort of like watching a scary movie and peeking at the screen between my fingers. I wanted to see what was happening, but it would lessen the blow by peeking just a little. I did this in the shower while looking down at the floor. I suddenly removed my fingers and almost screamed. Hair was floating around the tub. It looked like I had just washed a cat.

When I dried off, I barely touched my hair. I looked in the mirror and it didn't look *too* bad. A few hairs were out of place, but with enough gel and mousse, I could make anything look good. I removed the comb from the cabinet to straighten the section of hair that was out of place. When I ran the comb through, I realized just how out of place it really was. It was so out of place the entire right side of my hair fell out in the sink. *Well now, that's not good,* I thought. *I don't think I can make the gel or mousse work for me now. Maybe superglue. Screw it. No church for me today.*

I lay down on the couch and started crying. I was losing my hair, and it really hurt now. I called Sandra and asked if she would shave it for me. She said she would, so I called Vickie to see if she would go with me. When she got there, she asked me if I was sure I wanted to shave it. I didn't, but I didn't want to walk around looking like a mangy dog either.

Vickie, Brittany, and I went downstairs to Sandra's home. I sat down in the chair, and she got out her clippers. After the first pass over my head with the clippers, I was crying. So were Brittany, Vickie, and Sandra. What made it worse was her boys, ages seven and five, came in and laughed at me because I was getting my head shaved.

They said I looked stupid and asked me why I was doing it. I couldn't talk due to the hurt and embarrassment. Man, the honesty of children. Sandra told them that I was sick and the doctor said the only way I could get better was to shave my head. They seemed to be happy with that answer and walked off.

After my head was completely shaved, she asked me if I wanted to see it. I gave a very adamant *no*. Instead, I put on the skull cap and wig I had purchased. It wasn't until I had it on that I would look at myself in the mirror. I hated what I saw, but I guess it was better than having no hair.

We went back upstairs to my apartment, and Brittany and Vickie went to pick up something for dinner. I noticed that my head wasn't smooth and the skull cap hurt when I put it on. It was getting stuck on the stubble. I tried on a few hats I had purchased, but the problem persisted. So I grabbed the shaving cream and a razor and lathered up my head. I still didn't want to see what I looked like yet, so I shaved my head just by feel. After several swipes with a razor, my head was smooth as a baby's bottom. The skull cap, wig, and hat went on smoothly.

When Monday morning came, I was a little nervous about going to work. I was completely bald and would have to wear my wig. The wig was a little lighter in color than my natural color and quite a bit longer. It hit me right at the top of the shoulders and had bangs that went straight across my forehead. Brittany could tell I was nervous, so she looked at me and said, "Mommy, you look beautiful." I went to work with my head held high.

I got a few looks from people who were confused and wondering how my hair grew long so fast. However, no look was scarier than the one I got when I went to the post office one day at lunch.

In the military, we are required to remove our hat upon entering a building. That day, my hair came off with my hat. No wonder people were standing there looking mortified. I was standing there, bald as a cue ball, my hat in my hand and my hair still inside my hat. All I could do was put on my hat and walk back to my car. I was humiliated and cried all the way back to the office.

Once back in the office, I went in to talk to my commander about wearing my wig. I told him what had happened and how uncomfortable it was to wear. It was hot and made my scalp itch, even with the skull cap. I asked permission to wear civilian clothes and a hat until after I was done with chemotherapy and my hair came back in. He said yes without any hesitation.

I finally got comfortable being bald, but it was really hard for Brittany. She was embarrassed by it and always asked me to wear my hat or wig. One time we were driving somewhere, and I was hot—a horrible side effect of the chemo—so I decided to take my hat off. After passing a few cars and seeing those inside stare and point while laughing, Brittany begged me to put my hat back on. I was upset that she was more concerned about what people were thinking about me than what or how I was feeling.

In between chemo treatments, my hair started growing back in. All I could see were the hair follicles because they were dark brown. I looked like someone had taken a dark marker and put small dots all over my head. When the hair grew back, it would itch, which made me scratch my head a lot. Scratching my head a lot made it dry, so Sandra would come up once a week and massage my scalp with oil. What a treat that was!

One night Brittany was using the lint roller to get pet hair off the couch, and I made a comment about using it on my head to remove the dark hair follicles. She laughed but asked if she could try it. Why not? She started rolling the lint roller over my head and it worked like magic. Every tiny hair follicle was removed. This became a nightly ritual. What a sight it was—me sitting on the floor in front of Brittany, and her rolling a lint roller over my head. Just another fun thing to do that cancer had brought into my life.

Treatment # 2

Things were going well in my life, and I was starting to feel good. It must be time for the next round of chemo. I was told that when I started feeling as if I were at the top of my game, I needed to look at my calendar, because it was probably time for another session. Sure enough, my next round of chemo was only two days away.

On approximately February 19, I was back in the oncology department for treatment number two. I was checked in and weighed, and then my sister and I were led down the hallway. Just as I was turning to go into the chemo room, I was met by Rebecca. She stopped me and said I was going to be in one of the private rooms (dying rooms) today.

"Oh, no. Did he get my other test results back? Am I dying? How bad is it? How long do I have to live? What's going on? Why am I going into the dying room?" I shot these questions off so fast that she didn't even have time to answer.

Rebecca asked me to be patient and have a seat, saying she would be right back with me.

"No," I said adamantly. "I want to know what's wrong with me, and I want to know right now."

She looked at me, then Vickie. "Man, she's stubborn!"

"Yes, she is," Vickie replied.

I wasn't moving. I was standing there trying not to pass out. Rebecca took me by the hand and asked me nicely but firmly to get my ass in the room, sit down, and shut up.

I looked at her, somewhat hatefully I might add, and took a seat in the room. I was worried and on the verge of tears. I just knew I was dying. Vickie was trying to console me by laughing at how stubborn I was and how hard I was trying to look pissed off. "The look you were going for, well, you missed," she said. We both started laughing and stopped as soon as Rebecca came back in the room. She sat down and started laughing too. She said I was one of the most stubborn patients she had by far. I didn't find anything funny about being in the dying room, and I was getting madder sitting there being laughed at.

I sat there all huffy. Rebecca looked at me and said, "Kim, you're not dying."

"I'm not?" I asked. "Then why on God's green earth am I in the dying room?" It was then she told me something that solidified my thinking about how I was going to deal with my cancer from this day forward—with fun and laughter.

"Kim, people don't want to take chemo with you," she said.

I acted like I was sniffing my armpits. "I take showers, and I smell good. I also brush my teeth and use mouthwash."

"Frankly," she said, "you're too happy."

"What?" I asked. "Too happy? Is that possible? Of course I'm happy. Why wouldn't I be? I'm alive and I have people who love me very much. I'm happy because I've been given a second chance at life. I'm happy because cancer didn't kill me, and as long as I can breathe, I'll fight it so it won't. The last time I checked, having a positive and healthy attitude was one of the best ways to fight this disease. I don't care what they, or you, say for that matter. I'm taking chemo in that room with everyone else, and if they don't like it, well, then, they can leave."

I stood up, walked into the chemo room, took a seat, and made my presence known. Rebecca walked in, her eyes big as marbles, and started drawing my blood for the blood counts. She didn't say a word, nor did I. That was the quietest chemo session ever, but my blood was boiling. I wanted to smack every one of them in the face and tell them to wake up. I wanted to tell them that life was too short to be this way, especially now.

I guess they needed to wallow in their pity and let the whole world know how miserable they were. I guess they wanted me to wallow with them and be miserable too. I guess they didn't know me very well.

During this session Dr. Figgs came in and said he wanted to speak to me after my treatment. Great. First I had to hear that people didn't want to take chemo with me, and then Dr. Doom said he wanted to talk to me. This couldn't be good.

The treatment wasn't going well this time. I was really nauseous, and I had an instant headache. Maybe it was the stress, but something just didn't feel right this time. My back was hurting, and it felt like someone was sticking pins and needles in my spinal column.

> *HER2 positive tumors tend to grow and spread more quickly and are more aggressive than other types of tumors.*

After my treatment, I went in to see Dr. Figgs, and he told me he got the rest of my labs back. It turns out that not only was my tumor estrogen positive, it was also HER2 positive. HER2 stands for Human Epidermal growth Receptor 2. These tumors tend to grow and spread more quickly. Women with HER2-positive tumors have a more aggressive disease, greater likelihood of recurrence, poorer prognosis, and decreased survival rates.

He told me my cancer was very aggressive, and for someone so young, it was even worse. Because I was estrogen positive, I would have to have my ovaries removed as soon as I was finished with all four cycles of chemo. With my cancer being HER2 positive, it also meant I was susceptible to many different types of cancer, and I had a higher chance of recurrence.

He did have some good news, however. Since I had my breast completely removed and the cancer was only in two of my lymph nodes, I would not have to have radiation. We talked a little more, and he asked me if I understood everything he told me. I told him I would never be able to completely understand it, but I would have to trust him and take his word for it.

I wasn't expecting any different effects from my second treatment, so I was prepared. I would take my anti-nausea pills to keep from getting sick, lose my hair again, feel bad at times, and protect myself from the germs that waited to kill me.

I went home from the treatment completely wiped out. I wasn't this tired before, but I knew it could get worse with each treatment. I crawled into bed and took a nap until Brittany came home. Even though I was taking the pills that made me hungry, I didn't feel like eating. I just wanted to sleep. And I did. I went to bed around 6:00 PM and slept until the next morning when it was time for work.

Friday morning started out slowly. You'd think I would be excited to go to work because it was Friday and the weekend was in view. I was excited, but I couldn't get my brain and body to work together on the excitement. I just wasn't feeling well and couldn't get going. I didn't let Brittany see I was hurting or didn't feel well because I didn't want to scare her. I told her I was just tired because I didn't sleep well. She bought it and left for school.

The more active I was, the worse I started feeling. I got to work and was so weak it took me about twenty minutes to walk from my car in the parking lot to the office, which was normally a five-minute walk. I sat down at my desk, and my head felt like it weighed about fifty pounds. Before I knew it, I had my head down on my desk trying to type.

My commander walked by and came into the office. I apologized for not standing up (a big issue in the military) when he came in. He asked me what was wrong, and I told him I just didn't have any energy today.

"I want you to go home," he said. I looked up without saying anything. He said, "You don't have a choice, Kim. This is a direct order." One can get in trouble by disobeying a direct order in the military, so I started packing up to head home. "Call us if you need anything," he added.

I made my way back to the car and was so tired that I had to sit for a few minutes before driving home. When I got to the apartment building, I went inside and had to take a deep breath to start my climb to the fourth floor. I made it up about six steps and almost passed out. I couldn't breathe, and my legs were so shaky I had to sit down. I was so breathless that I couldn't call out to ask for help. So I stayed on my butt and scooted up a few stairs at a time. It took me almost thirty minutes to get to my apartment. When I got there, I sat down in front of my door and leaned against it. I was so exhausted that I fell asleep for about thirty minutes. I woke up, put my key in the door, opened it, and crawled inside.

I kicked the door closed and passed out on the floor from exhaustion. When I woke up, I realized I was in the middle of the hallway floor. I still had my uniform on, and my keys and purse were still in my hands. I had to go to the bathroom, so I pulled myself up and got myself to the bathroom and onto the toilet. My head was so heavy that I had to lean against the wall for a few minutes before getting up. I changed clothes, took my medicine, and hit the couch.

At that point I realized just how bad I felt and how bad I was hurting. There wasn't one part of my body that didn't hurt—my eyes, fingers, toenails, lips, tongue, and ears. It hurt to swallow, to eat, to blink, to touch anything, and even to hear. I pulled up the blanket and went back to sleep.

I woke up to my doorbell ringing. There was no way I was getting off the couch to go answer it. Then I heard keys in the door. I knew Brittany was going to her friend's house after school, so it could only be Vickie. She came in and was yelling for me. At that point I realized it hurt even to talk, so I stayed still and did nothing. She came into the living room saying how I could have at least answered her.

I told her how bad I was feeling, and then she understood. I started crying, and it hurt so much that I cried even harder. Vickie held me for a few minutes, and then I whispered, "Vickie, I quit."

"What do you mean, quit?"

"I'm quitting chemo," I said. "I don't care if I die. Let cancer kill me. I can't do this anymore. I won't do this anymore. I can't be alive if I'm going to feel like this. Just let me die." I must have said something that made her mad, because she jumped up and went into my bedroom. She grabbed an eight-inch by ten-inch picture of Brittany and brought it back into the living room. She put in on my chest about five inches from my face. I looked at it and turned away.

"No!" she said. "You look at this picture. Maybe *you* don't want to fight, but you need to fight for her. She needs you. You can't give up. It's not fair for you or her or the rest of your family. You're being selfish, and if you want to feel this way, I don't want to be a part of it."

I broke down and started sobbing. I needed to hear this. I needed someone to get mad at me and make me mad. "I don't want to die. I want to live. I'm sorry. I won't give up. I will fight. I promise you, I will fight." Vickie hugged me and left me to sleep.

When I woke up, I was still feeling miserable. I figured maybe a hot shower would soothe some of the pain. I turned on the water and got the temperature just right. I screamed when I got under the water because it felt like razor blades were slicing every inch of my skin. I started crying and wondered what was wrong with me.

I got out of the shower just about the time Brittany was getting home. She asked me if I was okay, and I told her I had a headache and took a shower to make it feel better. I think she knew I was lying. I just didn't want her to have to worry any more than she had to.

By Monday morning, I was feeling a little better, so I decided to go to work. When I walked in, my commander asked what I was doing at work and if I was feeling better. I thanked him for his concern and told him I wasn't great but better than on Friday. I had to be at work because I couldn't sit at home. I had to stay busy. He thanked me for my dedication, but he had no idea. He had no idea the reason I came to work every day was to escape the depression and sadness that surrounded me when I was home alone.

During the time between treatments, I went back to almost normal. The only thing different was that I had no hair and I was wearing civilian clothes. Often when we went out, I would wear a wig because of Brittany's feelings. She had become accustomed to my baldness, but the stares of others still made her uncomfortable.

One time when I went out to dinner, I ran into someone in the bathroom whom I hadn't seen in about six months. She hugged me and asked me when I decided to let my hair grow long. I reached up, pulled off my wig, and said, "Since I decided to do this." I thought she was going to pass out. I explained the whole thing to her, and she asked how I was *really* doing.

"I'm good," I said. "Things are different for me, but I'm handling it the best way I can. It's hard not having my hair, but it's harder not having my eyebrows and eyelashes. I can put on a wig to cover up my bald head, but there's not much I can do with my eyebrows and eyelashes. People think I'm crying all the time because I have no lashes to protect irritants from getting into my eyes. I also lost all the hair inside my nose, so I sneeze all the time. I guess the good thing is I don't have to shave my legs, armpits, or bikini area anymore because I lost all that hair too. But, hey, I'm just grateful to be alive."

She was amazed that I could feel this way after everything I'd been through. I couldn't figure out why she thought that. I'd always been a happy person, and I was trying not to let it change me, but in some ways I knew it was. I sometimes got depressed and took the attitude of "poor me." Even though it wasn't healthy to think that way, I felt I would be depriving myself if I did not allow my feelings to surface. In a way, it was good to get it out of my system when I was alone at night. I kept those feelings hidden from those around me who loved me and worried about my well-being.

Treatment # 3

Things were going well when I realized it was time for my third chemotherapy session. I was dreading this session because of how bad the last session had hit me. I just kept thinking, *I'm halfway across the finish line. Only one more to go after this one.*

I also was dreading this appointment because of how people reacted to me in the chemotherapy ward, especially those who thought I was too happy. Before leaving for the hospital that morning, I had Brittany write a message on the back of my head. It simply said, "I'm having a bad hair day."

Everything went like clockwork, except I almost didn't get the treatment because my blood count was only 401. Remember, if the blood count dipped to four hundred, I would be put in the hospital and given antibiotics to keep me from getting sick. Before she started my session, Rebecca had to check with Dr. Figgs to make sure it would be okay for me to continue with treatment.

He came in and talked to me about the possible repercussions of continuing this treatment with my blood counts so low. I could get really sick, and my body would not be able to fight infection. My body could shut down. I begged him to let me continue and told him I would take extra precautions to avoid germs. I didn't want to spend another month in that chemotherapy ward, so I was willing to forego the risks. He agreed and told Rebecca to prepare my treatment.

While I was waiting for my chemo to arrive, I put on my sunglasses and leaned back to watch the other people in the room. Most of them just sat there with blank looks on their faces, but some were reading or watching television. A few of them were watching me, probably to make sure I wasn't being "too happy."

My chemo arrived, and Rebecca sat down to push the medicine into my body. We joked around a little, but I was trying to be courteous of the feelings of those around me. After the Adriamycin was pushed and she hooked up the Cytoxan, I asked if I could go for a walk. She said yes.

On my way out of the chemo room, I made a comment about my being hot and asked Rebecca if I could leave my hat in the room. She said it would be fine, so I took it off and hung it on the coat rack and headed out the door.

As soon as I turned around to leave, everybody in the room busted out laughing. I turned around and said, "What? Do I have a hole in my pants?" Nobody said anything. They just looked at me and tried to keep from laughing. I turned back around to leave and once again the room was filled with laughter. I looked at Rebecca, who was laughing so hard she had tears in her eyes. "What's everyone laughing at?" I asked. She took me over to the mirror, gave me another mirror, and asked me to take a look at the back of my head. I pretended to be in shock as I read the words, "I'm having a bad hair day," written on the back of my head.

"Oh, my God," I said. "Brittany did this. When I woke up this morning she was sitting in my bed and was messing with my head. She said she was rubbing it for me. I can't believe she did this. Oh, man, she is going to get it when I get home." I looked up and everyone was still laughing.

The nurse asked me if I wanted my hat back, and I said that I'd better wear it on my walk. I put it back on and headed out the door. Rebecca came out after me and said, "Hey, Kim, wait a minute. You knew that was on the back of your head, didn't you?"

"Of course I did. I told you I'd get them to laugh one way or another. It worked."

She smiled and said, "Good for you." She high-fived me and off I went for my walk, but not before laying my hat back down. I figured if the patients in the chemo room could use the laugh, so could others in the hospital. It was funny. As I would pass people, I noticed that they didn't have the nerve to stare at me while facing me, but I could tell from their laughter they had turned around to stare at me behind my back.

I went back into the chemo room, and it was amazing how the people had changed. They were friendly toward me and laughing. That room was noisy, more than it had ever been. A few of them even thanked me for making them laugh. It's remarkable how quickly people changed when they realized that laughing and having fun was acceptable and just might make them feel better.

Rebecca finished with a few of the patients and got them on their way. I should have been the first one to leave, but she asked me if I could stay until everyone left. She wanted to talk to me. I said, "Sure. It's not like I have some hot date waiting for me." She laughed and looked at me with a look I had never seen from her before. It was strange.

When everyone had left, she came up to me and gave me a hug. "What's that for?" I asked. She said she wanted to hug someone who touched so many lives that day. I was at a loss for words.

"Kim, you have no idea how you helped those people in there today," Rebecca said. "Most of them didn't want to take chemo with you at first, and now they all want to be in the chemo room with you."

"I did nothing special. I was just being me."

"That's what I'm talking about. How can you continue to be so upbeat and positive all the time when you're fighting so hard to live? How do you not let it get you down? Do you ever let it get to you?"

"Don't come to my house after midnight," I told her. She gave me a puzzled look. "At night, when I'm home alone and Brittany has gone to bed, I allow myself to grieve and feel sorry for myself. I don't want, or should I say, won't, let others see me like this. I feel I have to keep up a certain appearance and attitude for everyone, and if they see me down or upset, I'll feel like a failure. It's hard because everyone thinks I'm so strong and brave, but I'm not. I have fears and tears just like everyone else. I'm so afraid of dying. I'm often afraid of going to sleep at night for fear of not waking up. I have to keep up this appearance because that's what people expect. I'm happy and I'm grateful I've been given this second chance at life.

"People ask me all the time why this happened to me. I wondered that too. I sometimes think it was due to my past or things I had done. I sometimes think it's because I didn't eat right or exercise enough. However, the one that gets me is when people asked why God gave me cancer. That got me to thinking. 'God didn't give me cancer,' I tell them. God let me find out about it when it was right for me. I'm living in a foreign country, far away from my family, but I'm with my sister. I work in a place where I have true friends whom I trust to look after me and Brittany. I'm at a military hospital in a foreign country that has an oncology ward inside the hospital. How much easier could this have gotten for me? No, God didn't give me cancer, but he sure was with me when I found out and surrounded me with people who could help get me through it. Furthermore, to be totally honest, I believe I have cancer to help someone else."

Rebecca had tears streaming down her face when I finished my dissertation. "I knew you had a secret about how you're dealing with this," she said. "Kim, you're a strong person, and you've shown us all so much. I've learned so much from you. And you have helped someone— you've helped me. I had breast cancer a long time ago, and the only way I dealt with it was anger. I got over it, but it took me quite a while to do so. If I had taken your approach, I think I would have been able to help more people than I do now and not have allowed myself to stay angry for so long. You are a true inspiration."

Then she said something I'll never forget—and which put me on the path I'm on now: "One day, you should tell your story. You'll help a lot of people." With that, we hugged, and I left.

The third treatment was almost like the first. I didn't get as sick as I did with the second treatment, but I was still extremely tired and run down. Because of the steroids in the anti-nausea medicine, I gained almost fifty-five pounds by the end of the third treatment. My face was puffy and my clothes didn't fit me well. I was uncomfortable, but I knew this side effect wouldn't last forever.

After this treatment, I noticed that I had trouble with certain foods I normally didn't have trouble with. For instance, I could eat spicy foods before, but now I would get severe indigestion immediately. Another problem was garlic. I loved garlic, and before chemo I could eat anything with garlic. After chemo, I still loved garlic, but it didn't love me. If I ate something with lots of garlic, I might as well park my behind in the bathroom, because that's where I would spend the next two or three hours.

So, once again, this disease that wasn't going to change me had changed my appearance, changed how I interacted with people, changed the way people treated me, and now had changed the way I ate.

Treatment # 4

The end of April was approaching, as was my last chemo treatment. The weather had started to get warmer, so we were spending more time outdoors. I was feeling better and wanted to get back to my routine of doing things around the house.

One Sunday, I was out washing my car to get all the grime off from the rain and snow. I started getting really warm, so I took off my hat.

> *I was afraid of taking chemotherapy treatment, but I was more afraid of stopping it.*

I wished I would have thought of sunscreen, because about three hours later my head looked too much like Rudolph's nose. It was so painful I had to give up my scalp massages for a while. I learned my lesson that weekend.

I was very emotional the week before my last treatment. I don't know why, but I cried easily. I wanted to hide out from people because I just didn't want to talk to anyone. I just wanted to be left alone.

When I showed up at the hospital, even Rebecca knew something was wrong with me. I was smiling and laughing, but not at the level I used to. I didn't want to talk to Vickie or play a card game. I just wanted to sit there.

Finally, Rebecca came over and asked me what was going on. She said it was my last treatment and I should be excited it was over. I should be jumping for joy.

"That's the problem," I told her. "I've been coming to this clinic for four months and getting a drug pushed into my body that's killing all the cancer cells. This is the last treatment. These drugs have been helping me fight for my life all this time, and now it's over. How long will it take for the cancer cells to realize my body is no longer being fed this drug? How long will it take for the cancer cells to start growing again? I was afraid of taking the treatment, but now I'm more afraid of stopping it."

She said it was normal and almost everyone that came in for their last treatment felt this way. She said it was the fear of the unknown and wondering when the other shoe was going to drop. "Kim, you're always going to wonder about your cancer coming back. Every new ache and pain will make you question. Every test and doctor's appointment will have you on pins and needles. You'll feel this way for the rest of your life. It might get easier, but it'll never go away. Trust me on this one."

I cried during most of the treatment that day. When I was done, I said good-bye to everyone and wished them all well. They all thanked me for being me and for bringing some sunshine into their chaotic life. It was a tearful good-bye to the staff, to Rebecca, and to Dr. Figgs. I hugged Dr. Figgs and thanked him for saving my life. He said, "I did nothing. You did all the work, and your attitude and beautiful spirit kept you going strong. Keep walking that path and you'll be fine."

I replied, "Doc, I love you, but I hope I never see you again."

With that, I turned around one last time to look at the chemo room, the staff, and the patients. A tear ran down my cheek as I turned and closed the door to the chemotherapy department for the last time.

The next few weeks were normal because I still had to go through the three weeks of the side effects of the chemo. The fourth treatment was like the second one in that I was so sick I couldn't function for days. However, it was more intense this time. There were days I couldn't even stand my clothes touching me. It was rough and I got through it, but I was scared.

I was scared of my new life and my new future. I had a new outlook on life, but I wasn't about to waste it. I had many challenges ahead of me now, the biggest being my pending hysterectomy. The second was my adjustment to living my life as a cancer survivor.

Chapter 12

Life after Chemo

In June 2002, I was up for my last reenlistment in the Air Force. I was happy because my hair was showing signs of starting to grow back, and I wanted to be in uniform when I reenlisted. My reenlistment date was set for Flag Day, June 14. I couldn't think of a better day to have this small but important ceremony.

My hair looked like it did when I first shaved it because it wasn't that long. I didn't care; after all I had been through, being able to stand up in front of the flag and reenlist to serve my country meant the world to me. As I was taking the reenlistment oath, I allowed myself to be proud of everything I had just been through.

When my hair began getting longer, it was funny because it was coming back in jet black and wavy. I had never had curly hair in my life, and it certainly was never black. I loved it because it also looked like it had been highlighted with gold streaks. Someone made a comment about my hair and how good it looked. Then she asked me who did it. "God," I said. After a few seconds of hesitation, she looked at me and said, "Where does he work?" I wanted to tell her if she didn't know that, then she had bigger problems.

One of the other issues I was facing was my promotion testing. In the Air Force, we have to test on job knowledge and military knowledge to get promoted to the next rank. My current rank was Technical Sergeant (E6), and I was testing for Master Sergeant (E7). If I made this rank, I would be put in the Top Three, the highest tier one can achieve in the non-commissioned ranks in the Air Force.

I should have tested in the January–March 2002 testing cycle, but since I was going through chemotherapy, I asked for and received permission to test out-of-cycle. This meant I could test after the normal testing cycle but before the new one began. I don't remember my exact test date, but I tested sometime in August.

In November, I was once again admitted to the hospital, but this time it was for a complete hysterectomy. I had to have only my ovaries removed due to the estrogen issue, but I decided on a complete hysterectomy. Since I had to have the surgery anyway, I figured, *Why not take everything now so I don't have to worry about cancer in those other areas later?* I even tried to get Dr. Jones, the OB/GYN doctor, to take my spleen, gallbladder, and appendix, but she wouldn't do it.

> *Dermoid tumors can be filled with hair, eyeballs, and teeth.*

Instead of the normal abdominal hysterectomy, she said that a vaginal hysterectomy would be a better option. She could remove everything through an incision in the vagina and not have to cut open my stomach, which meant the recovery would be a lot easier on me.

Dr. Jones wasn't sure of what she would find during the surgery because of all the issues I've had in the past with pain in my ovaries. We knew I had cysts from time to time, but the pain had continued to get worse over the years.

The surgery went smoothly, and I had to spend the night in the hospital to make sure I had no issues from the anesthesia. The next morning Dr. Jones came in to check on me and told me what she had found.

My left ovary was enlarged, but nothing out of the ordinary. My right ovary was a different story. The reason I had so much pain in my right ovary was because it held a tumor that was 5 cm. She called the tumor a dermoid cyst, or teratoma. This type of tumor is rarely cancerous, but is unique because it is made up of many different types of cells. Dermoids are formed from a single cell that can become anything in the body. Often they are filled with a greasy, fluid like substance, hair, teeth, and even eyeballs. She explained when she cut mine open it was filled with tons of hair. Gross!

Dr. Jones was pretty sure it was not cancerous, but the hospital would send it off to the Air Force Institute of Pathology just to make sure. After doing one last check, she let me go home to recuperate for the next eight weeks.

Staying home for that long proved challenging to me. I hate sitting at home with nothing to do. I played computer games and caught up on my movie watching, but it wasn't satisfying me. I needed more. I even begged my commander to let me come back to work early, but he said no. I promised him I would do nothing more than sit at my desk and type, but I was met once again with a definite no.

A friend of mine brought over some books from a series. He had seven of the thirteen books in the series. I started reading the books and loved them. I was finally getting into this staying-at-home-all-day-and-reading thing.

One morning around 10:00, my commander's secretary called and asked if I would be available to come in for a meeting around 1:00. I told her no, not because I didn't want to, but because I was in the middle of reading book number five in the series. She said it was an important meeting, but I told her I had asked the commander to let me come in before, and he wouldn't let me, so I wasn't going to come in now. Of course, I was only kidding and giving her a hard time. There was no way I would talk to her or my commander like that.

I asked her what the meeting was about, and she said it had to do with us moving and consolidating some of our offices in Italy, Greece, and Belgium. We had to start working on this now because the effective date of the moves would be January 2003. I told her I would come in under one condition: I would be allowed to go to these places to close them down. She laughed and said she would mention it to the commander.

I went to the meeting, which about ten people attended. We were talking about the locations affected and the logistical issues when there was a knock at the door. The commander told the person to come in. In walked a man from our unit. He said he was sorry to interrupt, but there was someone outside that needed to speak to him (the commander) immediately. We all started to get up to leave, but the commander said it was okay because he would go outside to speak to this person.

As he started toward the door, someone else came in the room, and I immediately recognized the voice. I looked up and saw Vickie, but she walked right past me. She hurried in and said, "I'm sorry to barge in on your meeting, Colonel, but I'm looking for my sister and I can't find her anywhere. I'm getting worried. She's supposed to be home on medical leave, but I called her and she's not here. I have something extremely important I need to tell her."

He looked at her and pointed to where I was sitting. She turned around and I started crying. I said, "What's the matter, Sis? Vickie, what's wrong?"

She had a strange look on her face, and then she turned to the commander and said, "I can't do this." She turned back to me and said, "Sis, I do have something to tell you, but it's good news." As she was speaking, she reached into her pocket and pulled out a set of Master Sergeant stripes. "I'm here to tell you that you were promoted to Master Sergeant."

Everyone in the room stood and began clapping. I was shocked. Vickie then thanked my commander for allowing her to be the one to tell me of my promotion. She addressed the people in the meeting: "I'm so proud of my baby sister. To have been through everything she's been through and still have the devotion to study for promotion and make it is a true testament to her dedication and strength." She then turned to me and said, "Kim, I have never been more proud in my military career than I am at this moment, to be able to present you with your stripes for promotion to Master Sergeant."

After everyone congratulated me, I sat back down to finish the meeting. However, there was no meeting. It was all planned and staged in order to get me there to let me know I had been promoted. My commander told me to go back home and enjoy the rest of my medical leave, because when I returned, I would have more important things to do since I was now an enlisted member of the Top Three.

My life continued, but there were a few obstacles along the way. One was the implant in my left breast. About a year after my initial cancer surgery, the saline implant was showing signs of deflating or moving. In addition, I had developed a large knot to the left of the implant underneath my left arm. The plastic surgeon thought it was a fluid collection from removing the drains too soon, but he said he could take care of it when he performed surgery to fix my implant.

We waited until I was well healed from the hysterectomy and scheduled my surgery for March 2003. The plan was to replace the implant with a larger one and liposuction the fluid buildup from underneath the arm. I did my pre-op paperwork for the hospital, and my surgery would follow in a few days.

Once again, Vickie was with me at the hospital for my surgery. There had been an emergency, so my surgery was delayed for a few hours. I hated waiting. I just wanted to get it over with, mainly because I was hungry. I had already been without food or water since 10:00 the night before, and it was now 9:30 AM. I was starving. So was Vickie. I told her to go ahead and get something to eat and drink if she wanted, but she said no. She didn't want to because it wasn't fair to me. She said she would go as soon as I was in surgery.

Someone finally came in and said I would go to the operating room within the next twenty to thirty minutes, so I went to the bathroom one last time. I told Vickie to go get something if she wanted, but again she said no. When I came back to the room, Vickie was gone. I couldn't believe it. She said she wasn't going to get anything to eat or drink, but she must have. I know I told her to, but how dare she?

I went over to the television and flipped through the channels, mumbling a few choice words under my breath. I couldn't believe she left to go get something to eat and drink. I walked around the room like I was ready to beat someone up. *Man, I love her, but I can't believe she did this to me.* I turned around quickly because I saw something to my right. Before I knew it or could stop it, I let out a blood curdling scream that brought the nurses running.

Vickie had hidden behind the door and pulled it close to her. There was a curtain covering the window, and she had it pulled over her head. Her face was pressed tightly against the window. We both started laughing so hard we couldn't talk. Tears were streaming down our faces from laughter, and all the nurses could do was stand and watch us. They were probably thinking we both had a little of my pain meds that morning. Once again, Vickie proved herself to be my rock by taking my mind off my surgery.

The surgery was successful, but not as simple as the doctor originally thought it would be. The pocket of fluid had hardened, so liposuction was not an option. Instead, the doctor ended up having to cut it out. My original surgical scar was only about five inches and only across the left breast. It now extended under my arm and all the way to my back. The upside was that it finally looked like my breast was back. It wasn't perfect, but it was a start. My body was healing nicely, and my hair was completely back in and healthier than before. I still had to get tested every month for the first six months to make sure the cancer was staying away.

One test didn't prove to be so lucky for me.

Chapter 13

The Other Shoe Dropped

I had gone in for a routine exam when a swollen lymph node was discovered on the right side of my neck. All my blood tests were normal, but it was still a cause for concern. Given my history, the doctor decided it was best to remove it so it could be tested.

The surgery was scheduled in May 2003, and it started out routinely. A nurse came in to start my IV, and that's where things went downhill. Unlike the other times that were difficult, this one was extremely difficult. The nurse had already stuck me nine times with no luck, and she was talking about putting in a central line. It was taking so long that the doctor came in to see why I was not prepped for surgery.

The nurse told him about the problems with the IV and the possibility of a central line. He said he was so sure the lymph node was nothing that it wasn't worth the risk of putting one in. However, he would try to get the IV one more time, and if he couldn't get it, he would cancel the surgery and let me go home.

> A central line is a tube that is placed through the veins into the main artery that returns blood to the heart.

He got it in the foot. I would rather go through childbirth again with no drugs and give birth to a fifteen-pound baby than have another IV in the foot. It took two med techs to hold my legs down so I wouldn't kick the doctor. As soon as the needle was in, they injected me with anesthesia so I wouldn't care. And I didn't.

When I woke up, I had a bandage around my neck, which freaked me out. I panicked, and the nurse tried explaining to me that it would be okay. I am extremely claustrophobic and felt the bandage was choking me. The sensation of not being able to breathe gets so bad that I can't even have an oxygen mask on. I can't wear turtlenecks or anything tight around my neck because I feel like I'm being choked.

She called the doctor and told him what was happening. He said that it would be okay to remove the bandage. When she did, I realized he had made a small incision, maybe three inches long on my neck, and stitched it up beautifully with glow-in-the-dark, bright blue thread. The other thing I noticed was a small drain coming from the incision that was attached to a small test tube. This test tube collected the excess fluid draining from the incision site. No wonder he had it bandaged. They didn't want me scaring the stuffing out of anybody.

I got up to use the restroom and forgot about the drain in my neck. When I bent over a little to sit down, the tube fell, and it was almost pulled out of my neck. The good thing about it being stitched in place was that it kept it from being ripped out. The bad thing about it being stitched in place was that it pulled the skin and ripped it a little around the stitches. I let out a scream and the nurse came running.

She helped me back into bed and told me she would let the doctor know what happened so he could check it. Before she called him, she took my blood pressure and was worried because it was 195/105. She couldn't believe it was so high. (Maybe it had something to do with the fact that I almost ripped my neck open.) She had me lie down and rest and took it again thirty minutes later. Not good. Now it was 200/110.

Now she was really worried and wanted the doctor there immediately. The doctor came busting into the room with a worried look on his face. I didn't feel sick and I couldn't understand what the fuss was all about. She told him about my blood pressure. He asked her to take it again, and it was still 200/110. The doctor grabbed the manual cuff and stethoscope and took it himself because he couldn't believe it was that high. It wasn't. It was 118/78. He asked the nurse to take it manually, and she got the same reading. Turns out the electronic blood pressure machine was not working. They let me go home.

I didn't really want to go out while I was healing due to the drain in my neck. I didn't mind the stitches, but it was hard to explain the tubing and the drain. I had to wear a shirt with a pocket on it so I could put the tube in the pocket and not have to carry it around.

My drain came out in about four days, but I had to keep the stitches in for another week or so. I did get lots of stares and questions about my neck. Two instances stand out.

One was a question: "What happened to your neck?" I had told the boring story so many times that I decided to spice this one up a tad. Keep in mind I was bruised around the incision with the bright blue stitches, and the entire top of my right hand and fingers were bruised from the many failed IV attempts.

So when I was asked what happened to my neck, I said that I was in a bar fight. That immediately stopped the person in his tracks, and he gave me an inquisitive look. "Don't stop now. Tell me more," he said.

"I was in a bar and saw the most gorgeous man I had ever seen in my life. Unfortunately, he was with someone. I was making eye contact with him, and he was doing a little flirting back. I walked up to him, got in between him and his girlfriend, and started talking to him. His girlfriend grabbed my arm, spun me around, broke a beer bottle on the counter, and slashed me on the neck."

The person couldn't believe what he was hearing. "Are you serious? She just cut you? Did you call the cops? What did you do?"

"Yes, she slashed me on the neck with a beer bottle," I replied. "My injury was fairly minor, and it needed only a few stitches, but I went home that night. However, she was not so lucky." Then I held up my hand for him to see the massive bruises on my hand and fingers. "She spent two nights in the hospital because I beat the crap out of her."

He couldn't believe it happened. "It didn't," I told him. "I made it all up because it sounds better than just saying I had surgery." It got a laugh, so I succeeded.

The second incident was even funnier. I was standing in line to get something to eat. There was a mom and her daughter—I would guess to be about six years old—in front of me. I noticed the little girl was staring at me, and then she leaned over to look at my neck. I smiled at her and looked away.

She finally asked me, "What's wrong with your neck?" Her mom gasped in horror and told her it was not nice to ask questions like that. The mom turned and apologized to me for her daughter. I told her it was no problem. Everybody in line snickered to themselves.

No sooner did the mom turn back around then the little girl said, "Are you sick? What's wrong with you? Why do you have a cut on your neck?" I thought the mom was going to pass out, along with everyone else in line. They were all holding their breath to see what I was going to say.

I looked at the mom, who was white as a ghost, and she mouthed the words, *I'm sorry*, and turned back around. The little girl turned to her mom and said, "But, Mom, why does she have a cut on her neck?"

The mom was now beet red and turned to look at me. The other people in line were not sure what to do. They were looking away and trying to keep from laughing. I told the mom it was okay and I didn't mind answering her question. The mom said, "Are you sure?"

"Yes, it's okay," I said. So the little girl asked me one more time. "So, why do you have a cut on your neck?"

Without any hesitation or emotion in my voice, I looked at the little girl and said, "Because I asked too many questions."

The mom turned around with a surprised look on her face, but gave me the "way to go look." The people in line couldn't take it anymore and burst into laughter. I felt bad for the little girl, who was still shocked at my answer, but it shut her up and she didn't ask me any more questions.

The next week I got the stitches out and was given the thumbs up. There was no cancer in the lymph nodes. It was only a residual infection from a recent sinus infection that had kept causing it to flare up. After a few weeks of antibiotics, I was as good as new.

Finally, my life had returned to normal and things were looking good. That was a sure sign for me to listen for the sound of the other shoe dropping. It did, but this time it had nothing to do with my health.

The shoe that dropped this time was in the form of a military transfer to Las Vegas, Nevada. I didn't want to leave Germany because my life was just getting started again, and I didn't want to leave all the people who became my family during my cancer crisis.

I talked to my commander about staying in Germany, but he could only guarantee me another year there. While that was okay for me, it would mean that my daughter would start high school and then have to move after the first year. I didn't want to put her through that because high school is hard enough.

After a great deal of soul-searching and talking to Brittany, we decided to accept the assignment and make the move to Nevada. It was hard saying good-bye to my friends because they had been there for me during a trying time in my life. However, I knew that no matter what, my true friends would never go away.

We arrived in Las Vegas on September 9, 2003. Our housing search started immediately, and we lucked out and found a nice townhome about a mile away from Brittany's high school.

In a way it was fun starting over and making new friends, but it was tough for me medically. I had to start my entire medical process all over again. Furthermore, it was a long process. First, my family doctor at the military hospital had to review my medical records. Then I was given an appointment with her. She repeated all the scans and blood tests. After she got all the tests back and reviewed them, I would be scheduled for appointments with the appropriate doctors.

During these routine scans, the doctors found a spot on my lungs that they continue to watch to this day. It's probably nothing more than scar tissue, but since it appeared after my cancer, they repeat the scan every six months to make sure it or nothing else is growing. I appreciate the scans, but sometimes I worry about the spot growing during that six-month span.

The first time I met my oncologist in Las Vegas, I fell in love with her. Dr. Ann was extremely nice and very thorough. During my first meeting with her, I learned so much about my cancer that no other doctor had told me about. She said she was going to draw a Cancer Family Tree. It was sort of like a Christmas tree, but we didn't want to have lights lighting up my tree. This tree would show who in both sides of my family had cancer. Unfortunately, my tree was pretty well lit up.

The one thing cancer patients should realize up front is that they need to trust their oncologist. If they aren't comfortable with the doctor at the first meeting, then they should find another one—and keep doing so until they find one that they trust with their life. I knew after our first meeting that I trusted Dr. Ann and knew she was doing the best thing for me. I told a friend of mine that I trusted Dr.

> *If you aren't comfortable with your oncologist, find another one and keep doing so until you find one whom you trust with your life.*

Ann so much that if she were to tell me to graze on cactus by a railroad track, I'd be there grazing within the hour.

Life was good. We were beginning to like Las Vegas. I was still in the military, and Brittany was nearing the end of her freshman year and loved high school. She had met a lot of great friends, and she was the ideal student and teenager.

In April 2004, I went in for a routine exam and was told I would need to have a mammogram to check to see how things were going. I had the mammogram done and was called back in for an ultrasound because of something the radiologist saw on the right breast.

The ultrasound showed about twelve to fourteen cysts in the right breast, and the radiologist questioned whether or not to do biopsies on them. There was no way in hell I was going to let them do fourteen biopsies. I wasn't going to go through that many needle sticks, and I was too afraid of what they might find. So I opted for the more drastic measure. I decided to have my right breast removed.

When I spoke to the general surgeon, he wasn't too keen on the idea, so it took some convincing. I told him I really wanted this surgery done because I didn't want to have to worry about getting cancer in the right breast. After many hours of being counseled by him on the surgery, he agreed to grant my request.

After the surgery was scheduled, I was also scheduled to meet with a plastic surgeon. He was extremely nice, but there were a few things he said that day that bothered me. First, he said that after the mastectomy, he could fix my large mastectomy scar and make it smoother and less noticeable.

"What scar?" I asked him.

He looked at me as if I were crazy. "The large scar across your left breast."

"Oh, that scar. Well, Doc, that isn't a scar. It's a lifeline," I said.

"Lifeline?"

"Yes. If I didn't have that line, I wouldn't be alive. It will always serve as a reminder for me to be thankful for every day that I wake up. I love my scar, and I never want it to go away."

Second, he asked me if I wanted to have my nipples reconstructed. I looked at him in astonishment. "Why?" I asked. He gave me some reason that I was young and single and I might meet someone some day. "Well, if I meet a guy and he's only worried about that, then he isn't the guy for me," I said. "Besides, it would be useless."

> *I don't have a scar; I have a lifeline.*

"Useless?" he asked.

"Doc, when the initial surgery was done and I had the mastectomy, they removed all of my nerves. I have no sensation or feeling on my breast anymore. Putting a nipple on me would be like putting a penis on your forehead." Immediately his face turned red, and he gave me a questioning look. I continued, "If you had a penis on your forehead, it would be for looks only. I'm pretty sure you couldn't use it, and you would get no pleasure out of having it there. That's what I feel about having my nipples replaced. It would be only for looks."

I think he wanted to question me more, but he knew better.

I met with my surgeon and plastic surgeon one last time, and we decided the surgery on the right breast would be a simple mastectomy, with no lymph node removal. If they saw something during the surgery that looked cancerous, they would go ahead and remove the lymph nodes just to be sure. I chose immediate reconstruction, but this time the surgeon would remove the left implant, which was saline, and put silicone implants on both sides.

I was excited about this for a few reasons. One, I would never have droopy, saggy, bounce-off-my-knees-when-I-walk boobs because they would be perky for the rest of my life. Second, I would never have to worry about the frozen food section. The third and best reason was no bra, no bra, no bra.

The surgery started as normal except for one problem. There were no implants. I was being wheeled back to the operating room when the doctor stopped the orderlies and told them that my implants had not arrived yet.

After a few hours of scrambling around, they found some implants locally, which were delivered to the hospital via Federal Express. Imagine the surprise of the driver if he had to open that package and announce what it was that he was delivering: "I have a delivery of two silicon boobs for a patient in room 303." That would have been a sight to see.

Woo-hoo! My boobs had arrived, and it was time for surgery. I was taken to the operating room, and the surgery went off without a hitch. They told me ahead of time I would have to stay in the hospital overnight and maybe an extra day, so I had visitors lined up and plenty of things to keep me busy, such as books and magazines to read.

After surgery, the first thing I remember saying was, "God, my boobs look huge!" That got a laugh out of everyone, and then I was back to sleep for the rest of the night. The next day I was allowed to get up and walk around. My sister Vickie happened to be in Nevada attending a seminar, so when she came to visit me that night, she asked me if I wanted anything to eat. I was given the "all clear" to eat anything I wanted. She went out and bought me a juicy Wendy's hamburger. It was the best hamburger I had eaten in a long time.

While I was eating, a good friend of mine showed up. After dinner we all got ready to go for a walk. I asked if I could go outside and it was approved. Just as we were getting ready to leave, the nurse said I needed to take my next dose of Toradol. Toradol is an anti-inflammatory used after surgery to reduce the pain and inflammation of surgery. I had already been given a dose in the recovery room, and it did an awesome job in removing the pain without making me feel groggy.

The IV had been removed, but I still had the hep-lock in, so as I was walking past the nurses' station, a nurse stopped me to give me my dose. As soon as she started putting it into the hep-lock, I complained of intense pain. I asked her to stop because it felt like my veins were being ripped open from the inside. I turned around to Vickie and was crying due to the pain. "Please make her stop," I said to Vickie.

Sensing my panic, the nurse pushed the rest into the hep-lock in about five seconds and said, "There. You're all done. See, it wasn't too bad."

I walked off rubbing my arm due to the pain and giving the nurse a look that could have dropped her on the spot. We got into the elevator, and I started feeling sick. I told Vickie I wasn't feeling well, but we thought it must be the elevator ride and I would be fine when I got outside. The elevator doors opened and I stumbled out. Everything around me was fuzzy, and I started to get a loud ringing in my ears. I remember being led to a place to sit, and as soon as I sat down, I started getting the dry heaves. That's the last thing I remember.

The rest of the story comes from my recollection of what Vickie said happened. She said I started dry heaving and my head was rolling around like I had no muscle control in my neck. I was drooling and kept asking them to stop blowing the whistles in my ear. My friend went to get a wheelchair because by this time I couldn't walk, and I had no control over my arms and legs. They wheeled me back to my room and helped me into bed. Vickie said the nurse asked her what happened to me because I was doing so well when I left. Vickie said, "That's what I'd like to know."

I was out the rest of the night. When the doctor came in the next morning, he asked what happened. I told him the only thing I could remember was the injection of Toradol.

When I came home from the hospital, I started doing some research on Toradol and ended up calling the drug manufacturer. I spoke to a pharmacist at the company about the drug to see if I had an allergic reaction or if something else was wrong. What I learned was a shock and could have cost me my life.

The drug is not meant to be injected but infused with an IV over a fifteen- to thirty-minute time period. The entire injection of Toradol was pushed into my hep-lock in less than one minute without diluting it. Boy, was I pissed off at that point.

On Monday I saw my plastic surgeon for a follow-up and told him what had happened. He was outraged and lodged a formal complaint for me. Three days later the general surgeon called me and was mad at me for telling my plastic surgeon. He said, "One of my best nurses is now in a lot of trouble and no longer works in the clinic due to your complaint."

I told him that if she was one of his best nurses, then the hospital is in a serious predicament. She was unprofessional and complacent. Furthermore, I was glad she was gone.

The healing this time was going great; I was having no major issues. I kept up with my follow-up appointments, and I must say that my new boobs looked better than before. They were perky, round, and huge. For the first time in my life I had really nice cleavage. Things were looking up and going my way, until I went to see my dermatologist in July.

My dermatologist found a spot on my leg that he was not happy with. It was a small, red dot that didn't grow but was getting redder with each passing day. The dermatologist did a shave biopsy, and it came back as melanoma in situ. That meant it was melanoma, but it hadn't spread beyond the tissue removed in the biopsy. The recommendation was to cut a 6 mm section of tissue out around the original biopsy site, to which I agreed. Now I have this lovely scar on my leg, but I'm grateful for that scar because there was no more cancer in that chunk of flesh.

Once again, I was finally done with doctor appointments for a few months. My next one was in November 2004 with my oncologist, Dr. Ann. I went in for a routine appointment, and she started asking me questions that she normally didn't ask, such as, "Are you feeling okay? Have you been sick or had a sinus infection? Have you been more tired than normal lately?" Then she looked over at Brittany, who had just turned fifteen, and asked her if she could drive yet.

I knew something was up, so I asked her what was going on and why was she asking all these questions. She looked at her assistant and asked her to take Brittany into the waiting room. I said, "No, she's fine. Whatever you have to say to me you can say in front of her. She's been through all this with me."

She said that my platelet count was low—so low, in fact, that if I were in a severe car accident I could bleed to death before anybody could help me. Then she said she wanted to do a bone marrow biopsy. I said okay and asked when she wanted me to schedule it. She said, "You don't understand. Your platelet count is so low that we need to do it today. You're not leaving until we get it done." I asked her what she thought was going on, and she said she thought I had leukemia.

Dr. Ann's staff called my insurance company, and it was approved immediately. Brittany was asked to sit in the waiting room because the doctor didn't want her to watch the procedure. After it was over, I understood why.

I was asked to pull my pants down just below my waistline and lie down on my stomach. Dr. Ann numbed an area on my hip just above the left butt cheek. Then she took an instrument that looked like a corkscrew and stuck it through my hip down to the bone. I felt it hit the bone and almost threw up. The object was to get the corkscrew down into and through the bone to the marrow. To do that takes force. My doctor is a petite woman and had trouble getting the needle into the bone. The pain was so bad I lost feeling in my hands and arms from gripping the end of the table so hard. Believe it or not, it was a relief when she broke through the bone, but the sound was a different story.

Once into the bone, she showed me the needle she would use to aspirate the bone marrow. She held it up, and I commented that it wasn't a needle; it was a metal straw, because that's how big in diameter it was. She put that needle into the hole and proceeded to suck out the bone marrow. I know this might be hard to believe, but I could feel the marrow being pulled up the inside of my bone and into the tube. It felt like my body was being turned inside out during this process.

After the bone marrow extraction I thought I was done. No. Dr. Ann said she had to get an actual sliver of bone. I could only imagine what she was going to use to do that. She showed me the instrument. It looked like a long metal stick with a cheese slicer on the end of it. She went into the same hole again and took a tiny sliver of bone. It felt like my bone was being split apart at the seams. By this time I was crying so hard I couldn't catch my breath. The nurse made a comment to Dr. Ann that they were probably off my Christmas list now because of all the pain they were causing me. "You bet your ass you are," I said.

I had to turn over and lie on my back for twenty minutes before I could get up. They went and got Brittany and let her come back in the room. The assistant came in with a box full of needles and tubes because Dr. Ann wanted to do more blood tests. I looked at her and asked her just how much blood she needed. She looked and said, "Eighteen tubes, to be exact." I almost passed out.

As I was leaving, Dr. Ann asked that I come back in one week to get the results. "We don't give results over the phone," she added. I made the appointment for one week. When I stood up to walk, the pain was so intense I nearly fainted. I couldn't take pain medicine because I had to drive home, and we lived almost thirty minutes away from the doctor's office.

I stopped in the bathroom on my way out of the building and started crying. *This can't be happening again*, I thought. *I can't do this again.* Brittany held me tight and said it would be okay. She told me to have faith, but it was hard. I was beginning to question my faith. On my way to the car, I called my sister Lori to tell her what was going on, and she told me the same thing—to have faith. *Why is everybody telling me this? I know the results are going to be bad, and I don't want to have faith right now. I won't have faith right now.*

As we were pulling out of the parking lot and making our turn to go home, Brittany said, "Mommy, look." I looked at her, and she pointed up at the sky. There was the most beautiful rainbow I had ever seen. "See, Mom, it's going to be okay." I wanted to believe her, but the pain I was feeling at that moment was telling me otherwise.

As soon as we got home, I took a pain pill and a nap. When I woke up and tried to get off the couch, pain shot through my hip, making me fall back down. I started crying, but not from pain—from fear.

Brittany came over to the couch, held me in her arms, and kept telling me it was going to be okay. I sobbed in her arms and told her, "Brittany, I'm so scared. I don't want to have cancer again." This was the first time since my initial cancer ordeal that I admitted or showed fear to my daughter.

During the week leading up to my results, I did a great deal of soul-searching. I was mad because I felt like it was happening again. I was losing control to something that might be invading my body again. I wanted to run away and ignore what was happening, but I knew that would be a stupid decision. I had to face it head-on and fight again if I needed to.

For moral support I called a good friend of mine who is very religious and believes in the power of prayer. I told him what was happening and that I was really worried about this. He told me, "Kim, remember God doesn't put on you more than you can handle."

"I know," I said, "but should I remind him that I've had enough?"

I got my results back on Thursday. I took the day off because I didn't want to deal with anyone at work. I was driving Brittany to school that morning, and we were arguing about her going with me to get my results. I didn't want her to go, and she was insisting. "No, Brittany, you're not going with me and that's final," I told her.

"I am going with you, Mom, and that's final," she shot back. Then she reached over and turned up the stereo. I started laughing because I knew I wasn't going to win this one.

I dropped her off and told her I'd pick her up after school. She hugged me and said, "I love you, Mom." She hopped out of the car and disappeared into the crowd. I was headed home to get some stuff done before picking her up that afternoon. When I pulled away from the school, I had to cross three lanes of traffic to get into the left-hand turn lane to head home. As I was pulling into the turning lane, a car cut me off and pulled in front of me. *He must be in a hurry,* I thought.

I looked at the car. It was a gold car, perhaps a Chrysler Sebring. I looked at the license plate, which said MYFAYTH. *Wow,* I thought to myself. *Maybe it's a sign.* It didn't matter anyway. I just knew that something was wrong. I just knew I was going to begin my battle all over again. Good things didn't happen to me. Why should it be any different now?

The next thing I knew I was at another stoplight, and the same car is in front of me. Yep, same car, gold car, male driver, yep plates are ... oh, my God! The plates are different. It's the same car and same driver, but the plates now have TOLIVE on them. I must be dreaming. But I wasn't because the driver behind me was honking the horn because I wasn't moving. What was going on?

I pulled over to the side of the road in tears. I got it now. It *was* a sign, a sign from God that it would be okay and that I had to turn things over to him. I couldn't keep control anymore. It was *his* will, not mine. God sent me those signs when I needed them most.

When I got home, I called my friend and told him what had happened. He said, "See, I told you. Just turn things over to God and let him have control. He sent you a sign just like I said he would, and he probably has before, but this time he had to really get your attention."

"He's got it," I said. I said it, but deep down inside I still didn't know if I meant it.

When Brittany and I got to the doctor's office that afternoon, I walked inside and took a seat. When the nurse came out and called another patient, she acknowledged my presence with only a nod. She also had a sad look on her face.

"They're going to give me bad news," I said to Brittany.

"Why do you say that, Mom?"

"Did you see how she looked, or should I say, didn't look at me? She's always friendly and joking with me, and now she can't even look at me. It's really bad."

"Mom, chill out," was all Brittany said. A few minutes later the nurse called me back to the room and once again hardly spoke to me. She put me in an exam room and closed the door. A few minutes went by and nothing happened.

Then Dr. Ann burst into the room and said, "You're clean. There's no leukemia, and better yet, there are no breast cancer cells in your bone marrow."

"See, Mom," Brittany said.

I hugged the doctor and the nurse and told them both they were back on my Christmas list. After a few minutes Dr. Ann said, "I'll see you in six months."

I did it! I made it to the point where I could go six months between follow-up appointments. This is one those milestones every cancer patient longs for. However, my elation would be short-lived.

Chapter 14

No End in Sight

In early 2005, I began having intense pain in both breasts. It was so bad I couldn't even stand to wear a bra. Anything that touched my breasts felt like razors slicing my skin. In addition, they were hard as rocks and it hurt to breathe. Anything that put pressure on the breasts made it worse.

I was beginning to worry, so I went back to see my family doctor, who said I needed to see a plastic surgeon. She said it felt as if I had developed a severe case of capsular contracture, in which scar tissue hardens and squeezes the implant. This makes the implant feel very hard, and the breast may take on a ball-like appearance. I was told that I would need to go see a civilian doctor because the only plastic surgeon at the base had retired. The problem was further compounded in that no plastic surgeon in the state of Nevada took my insurance.

In July, I was sent to a doctor in La Jolla, California. Dr. Modelle agreed the implants needed to come out, but he would not put them back in because the capsular contracture would happen again. He offered me two procedures: one was the TRAM flap procedure (see chapter 8), which I had already heard about, and the other was the latissimus dorsi flap procedure. This procedure uses the skin, fat, and muscle from the upper back. It's tunneled under the skin to the front of the chest. This sounded like a great procedure, so we scheduled the surgery for mid-October.

I was to return in late September for a couple of days to get all my pre-op work done, such as labs and X-rays. I would also meet with Dr. Modelle again to finalize the surgery details. I arrived in La Jolla and met with the doctor later that same day. He ordered the labs and X-rays, and I was free to go back to my hotel. The next morning I would return to have all the tests done.

On my way back to the hotel, I received a phone call from my leasing company in Las Vegas telling me the owner of the town home I was living in had decided to put the town home up for sale. I had to be out by the end of October when my lease was up. Great. There was no way I could have this surgery and then head back home to try to move. I didn't know what to do. I needed to have this surgery, but I needed to move too. I hardly slept that night.

> *The latissimus dorsi flap procedure uses skin, fat, and muscle from the upper back, which is tunneled under the skin to the front of the chest.*

The next morning I stopped in Dr. Modelle's office to seek his advice. He advised me not to have surgery if I had to move. There was no way I would be healed in time to undergo a household move. So I canceled my surgery and took the next flight back to Las Vegas.

Instead of healing from surgery, I was now faced with the task of finding a place to live. I wanted to stay within my daughter's school district because I didn't want her to have to change schools. The leasing company had a place on the street behind us, so we went to look at it. I was warned that the prior tenants had been evicted, so we weren't sure of the condition of the house.

We walked into the house and almost walked right back out. It was disgusting; I think the previous tenants did everything they could to trash it before they left. There was food thrown all against the walls and all kinds of crap ground into the carpets. The place smelled disgusting, and they decided to break whatever fixtures were in the house.

We didn't need to think about it; our answer was no. We left, figuring we'd keep up our search. We headed back to our street but took a different route home. When we turned the corner to our street something caught my eye. It was like a beacon of light shining from the windows. It was a "FOR RENT" sign. My daughter immediately called the number and asked the gentleman who answered if we could stop by and look at the property.

"How did you know I had a place for rent?" the man asked. Brittany told him we had seen the sign in the window. He was stunned because he had just put the sign in the window and turned around when his phone rang. Divine intervention, I tell you.

We walked in and immediately asked him how much he wanted for rent. He told us the amount and asked if we wanted to look around. I told him no. "We'll take it," I said. I explained to him that I lived five houses down, and it was the exact same floor plan we were living in. I signed the paperwork that night. We had found a new place to live.

I waited until after we had settled into the new place before calling to reschedule my surgery in La Jolla. It was now mid-November. Imagine my surprise when I was told that Dr. Modelle dropped my insurance company from his practice. They operated on the government fiscal calendar, and when the new fiscal year started, the doctor's office started its new plans; my insurance company was no longer a part of it. I was devastated. I had to start back at square one.

I was able to get an immediate appointment with my family doctor. She cried when she heard about all the trouble I was having. She helped me get an immediate appointment with the plastic surgery clinic at a military facility in Texas. I would have to travel again, but at least I could stay within the military system.

In December I boarded a plane bound to meet with yet another plastic surgeon. The trip was worth it because this doctor was one of the best plastic surgeons I had met. He took the time to listen to my concerns and fears before suggesting the type of surgery that would work best. He suggested the TRAM flap procedure, and I agreed. I loved the idea—I got a boob job and a tummy tuck at the same time.

We scheduled the surgery for January 3, 2006. I had to travel on the January 2 to get everything ready the day before the surgery. Vickie, who was now living in Fort Worth, Texas, flew in and met me at the airport. She would stay with me that night, go with me until I got into surgery, go home, and come back when I was ready to leave the hospital. Vickie, my rock, was there to keep me calm and mellow the night before surgery.

Well, she tried to keep me calm, but mellow was not a part of our night. We had a nice dinner and then she took me to a place called Howl at the Moon, which is a dueling piano bar.

It was early when we walked in, and the musicians were just getting started. We sat and listened for a few minutes as they were practicing and warming up. The crowds started pouring in, and it was beginning to get fun. The piano players were on stage and getting the crowds into the music by telling us to come up with some songs. One of the performers said that if we were there to celebrate a birthday, wedding, birth, anniversary, divorce, or graduation, we should let them know so they could celebrate with us. Then he said, "Hell, even if you're here to celebrate having plastic surgery, let us know, and we'll celebrate that too."

My jaw hit the floor, and I immediately looked at Vickie. She was just as shocked as I was, or at least was pretending well. She grabbed the pen and notepad from our table and began writing. "You wouldn't dare," I said. She slid the paper over to me. It said, "Kim is having breast plastic surgery at 6:00 AM tomorrow morning." I couldn't believe she had written that down. So I wrote on it, "Because of cancer," and she handed it in.

It had been almost thirty minutes since we turned in the paper, and so far they hadn't picked on us. A few minutes later they turned all the lights down and brought up a big spotlight. *Oh, God, here we go.* A guy stood up on stage and asked, "Is Kim in the house with us tonight? Where's Kim?" My lovely sister helped point me out, and the spotlight was on me in an instant.

"Why don't you join me up on stage, Kim?" he asked. The crowd was getting into it and cheering me on. I couldn't say no at that point. I went up on stage, and he had me sit down beside him on the piano bench. The spotlight was turned on us, and he began to serenade me on the piano. It was embarrassing because he made up a sexual song about me and it wasn't very nice. When the guy finished his song, the crowd went wild and gave me a standing ovation.

That made my night and certainly took my mind off my surgery. We left the bar around midnight and headed back to the hotel. I wanted to take a shower and try to get some sleep because I had to be at the hospital at 5:00 the next morning, which came way too early.

We arrived at the hospital and I was checked in right away. The staff wanted to get me in early because my surgery was going to take a long time; therefore, a great deal of pre-op was still required that morning. I was really nervous and started crying when it was time for the IV. Vickie held my hand, and I asked for a chaplain before continuing. I was given a sedative and don't remember anything else.

The surgery lasted nineteen hours, and I was so drugged up on pain meds that I didn't remember anything for at least thirty hours after my surgery. I remember waking up and feeling overwhelming pain. My stomach felt like someone was dragging a hot match across my bikini line.

I was in and out of consciousness for the next few days, but one thing I do remember is looking at my left breast when the bandages were changed. I remember seeing a large, black spot on the breast and thought it was a bruise. When I was a little more coherent, the doctor told me some of the skin and tissue he transferred in the surgery didn't take. The black spot I was seeing was dead tissue.

I lay in bed and watched him cut a one-inch chunk of flesh out of my breast. I didn't feel it, which was weird. He didn't stitch it up—just packed it with moist gauze that had to be changed twice a day. He said it would heal itself from the inside out. It eventually did, but I had to change it twice a day for almost six weeks.

For the first three days, I wasn't allowed to get out of bed. It was driving me mad because my roommate had free reign of the hospital. I was finally allowed out of bed, but only to sit in the chair. That was hard because my stomach had been filleted from surgery; I had a cut from hip bone to hip bone. The next day I found out how hard it was to walk.

The time I spent in the hospital was tough. It wasn't like my hospital stay in Germany. At least there I was with friends, but in Texas I was alone. I didn't know anybody, and Vickie wouldn't be back for another week. I was getting very depressed and didn't want to get out of bed.

The doctor came in and said I needed to get up three times a day to walk. I didn't think it was possible, but it happened a little at a time. I got to where I was walking four times a day and eventually worked up from walking around my room to walking a complete circle around the nurses' station.

Things were going great. The doctor came in on Thursday and said if I kept improving, I could check out the hospital a few days early. However, I would have to stay in Texas until I got my drains out and my final checkup. I was excited but scared. Vickie wasn't coming back for a few more days, and I wasn't sure how I was going to take care of myself in a hotel room.

On Sunday, my doctor said things were looking good and I would be able to leave the hospital on Monday. The staff took out my IV and let me have free rein around the hospital. I took a hot shower and ordered a cheeseburger for dinner—not very healthy but much better than Jell-O. I walked the floor a few times and then headed to bed.

When I woke up on Monday, I was excited, but a little apprehensive, about being able to leave the hospital. I didn't feel great that morning, but I thought it was because I was nervous. My stomach was bothering me, and I ended up having diarrhea. I got back into bed, and when the nurse came in, I was covered up to my nose in blankets and told her I was freezing. She took my temperature and it was 103°.

She gave me Tylenol and washed me off with a cool cloth. I went to sleep, but my sleep wasn't restful because I was freezing. When I woke up, the nurses took my temperature again, and it had only dropped two degrees. They gave me another dose of Tylenol and a shot of antibiotics to ward off what might be trying to take hold of my body. I was told I could not leave the hospital until my fever was gone, so I spent another night in the hospital. I ran a fever most of the night and had diarrhea off and on.

When I woke up the next morning, the doctor came in and checked my incisions and drains to make sure I had no immediate signs of infection. They were clean. My temperature was back up, but this time it was 103.7°. He immediately ordered the IV be put back in and then had the nurses draw nine tubes of blood for cultures. I also had to provide a stool sample and a urine sample for them to culture.

My doctor thought I might have blood clots in my legs, so they sent me down for a venous Doppler scan of both legs. I couldn't sit in the wheelchair, so I was wheeled in my bed down to the radiology department. I was so out of it from the fever I don't remember the scan.

There were no clots in my legs, but my doctor still didn't know what was causing my fever.

That afternoon my fever dropped to 100°, but no matter what was tried, it wouldn't break. I was having trouble breathing, so the doctor thought I might have pneumonia. He ordered an immediate chest X-ray, and once again I was wheeled from my room to the radiology department.

Unlike the ultrasound, I was wide awake for this series of X-rays. The male nurse who took me down to radiology had been with me all week and was aware of my surgery and the reason I had it. The med tech who came out to do my chest X-ray was a young man new to the military. He was shy and very nervous.

When women have a chest X-ray, we are given two little metal dots to put on our nipples. The nipples are marked so they don't show up as dark spots on the film. The young man came over and gave them to me, and I just looked at them. He said, "Ma'am, I'm sure you know what to do with these."

I looked at them again and said, "No, I don't believe I do. I have no idea what these are for."

The young man began to stutter while trying to explain to me what those little metal dots were for. "Well, you put those metal things on your ... um ... well, you put them ... um, you put them ... well, on your nipples."

"Oh, I see," I said. The young man was relieved and his face was red as could be. Then I said, "I don't have any nipples."

He turned around and looked at me. Once again, he stammered through his words. "You don't ... um ... you don't have any ... um ... you don't have any nipples? Are ... are you sure?"

I pulled out my gown and looked down into it at both breasts. "Yep, I'm pretty sure."

My male nurse started laughing and said, "Kim, quit messing with him." He then looked at the med tech and said, "She's just messing with you. She had a double mastectomy due to breast cancer and doesn't have any nipples." Fun sucker.

After the X-ray, I was wheeled back to my room. We laughed all the way back. He said I was one of the funniest and carefree patients he had worked with in a long time. He said it was good to see patients have fun and be happy because it helped in their recovery. With everything I had been through, I couldn't agree more.

Wednesday arrived and I was still in the hospital. My tests all came back normal, and the blood work showed no signs of infection. However, I couldn't leave until my temperature was normal for twenty-four hours. That night, I woke up around 10:30 and was soaking wet. I paged the nurse, who came in to check my temperature. The fever had finally broken.

Vickie returned on Thursday, and I was so excited to see her. I started crying when she walked in the door because I had been so alone and depressed. She stayed in my room until almost midnight, when she left to go get some sleep.

On Friday, I was discharged. Before I left, the rest of my drains were removed. The only thing I had left was the hole in my chest where the doctor had cut out the dead tissue. We stayed in the hotel all weekend and watched movies. I read several books, and took a short walk every evening.

I had to go back and visit the doctor on Monday. He said things were looking great, so I asked him if I could go back home to Las Vegas. The hole was still pretty large in my chest, and he didn't want me to leave until that was healed. I begged him to let me go home. I told him my daughter was home in Las Vegas alone, and I wanted to get back to her. I began crying, and he agreed I could travel home as long as I saw a general surgeon to check on the hole in my chest as soon as I got back. I agreed.

I changed my reservations and headed to the airport the next day. The doctor wrote me a letter on my behalf stating that I needed to pre-board due to a medical condition. About forty-five minutes prior to boarding, I took two pain pills so I could sleep the entire flight. I got on the Southwest flight and sat in the front row. It was a full flight. When a passenger sat down beside me, I apologized to him up front for my possible fidgeting during the flight. He said it was no problem. We both made a comment to each other that we both thought each other looked familiar.

The flight took off and I went to sleep. The next thing I knew the captain was announcing that we were making our descent into Las Vegas. The guy sitting beside me began talking, and we were still trying to figure out how we knew each other. He said he did drywall for his normal job but dabbled in music in the evenings and on weekends. He said he and his buddy (who was sitting further back) were going to Las Vegas for the weekend for some training. We chatted until we pulled into the gate. The flight attendant came back with a wheelchair and escorted me off the plane.

I was waiting for airport services to take me to baggage claim to meet my friend who was picking me up. I was sitting alone when the passenger I was sitting beside on the plane came up and wished me good luck in my recovery. He walked off and hooked up with his buddy. When his buddy turned around, it hit me. He was the guy who pulled me up on stage at the Howl at the Moon bar in Texas. What a small world!

I made it home, where my baby girl was waiting with open arms. It was so nice to be home with her and to feel her close to me again. I had been gone for eighteen days. It was so good to be back. I had a long recovery ahead of me, but being at home, surrounded by people who loved me, helped.

Three months later, I had to go back to Texas to for an appointment with my plastic surgeon to see how things were healing. He said it was looking good, and I was done as far as he was concerned, unless I wanted to have my nipples reconstructed. I told him the penis story, and he shut up.

Since that surgery I've had a few more rounds of touch-up plastic surgery to try to perfect my breasts. I finished the last surgery and was at my last follow-up appointment when my doctor asked if I wanted to have my nipples redone. I went home and told Brittany what he asked, and she said, "Uh-oh, Mom. You didn't mention the penis thing did you?"

I started laughing. "No, honey, I thought I'd take it easy on this one … at least for now."

Chapter 15

Other Cancers in My Life

How amazing and powerful one word can be. *Cancer* is just one little word, but it can, and will, scare the shit out of you. It's a word that will stop you on a dime. Cancer is not prejudiced in any way, shape, or form. It doesn't care about your nationality or race. It doesn't care about how much you weigh or what your IQ is. Cancer doesn't care about those things; it just wants a place to grow and survive.

I promise you that if you ever hear the words, "You have cancer," you will make changes in your life. You might make these changes—such as eating healthier, stopping smoking, stopping drinking, and exercising more—based strictly on the fact that you have cancer. However, the vast majority of your changes will be internal. There will be changes in how you deal with people and in your priorities. You also will want to cut some things out of your life. These things are like other cancers.

That cancer might be your job, which is sucking the life out of you without giving you anything in return. That return could be job satisfaction or money. The job could be in a stressful environment. Perhaps you work with people who are always unhappy or negative. Or the opposite could be your problem.

Maybe you love your job so much that you want to spend as much time there as you can. You believe you can make a difference. You want to make a difference. You're so dedicated to your job and your boss that you give it your free time too. That's how I was. I loved my job in the military, and I loved my commander. My normal work hours were 7:30 AM to 4:30 PM, but I worked from 6:30 AM to around 6:00 PM. I needed to be there in case something had to be done right away.

When I was diagnosed with cancer, it hit me. If I died, anyone could come into the office and do the same job I was doing. My replacement could possibly do it better. But nobody could come into my daughter's life and replace me as her mother.

I cut that cancer out of my life. Yes, I still went to work and did my job, but I worked the normal hours just like everyone else did. The job didn't suffer and my commander didn't think differently of me. My friends and coworkers still liked me. The only thing that changed was I became closer to my daughter because we had more time to spend together.

It could be that a cancer in your life is your lifestyle. Maybe you're a smoker or a drinker. Maybe you burn the candle at both ends until there is nothing left to burn. Maybe you could buy stock in a fast food company because you eat at one of those places three to four times a week. These things didn't necessarily cause your cancer, but they are like a cancer in that you know you need to get rid of it and change your way of living. There is nothing like a cancer diagnosis to get you to wake up and turn your life around. You stop drinking and smoking, you eat a little healthier, and you start an exercise program. You feel that this is just another step to take in the battle against this disease that is waiting to rob you of your dignity, your pride, and possibly your life.

Another cancer in your life might be an unhealthy relationship. It could be with a friend, a lover, or even your family. You should either mend this relationship or cut it out of your life. This was a tough one because I've always been a "yes person," wanting to please everyone. There was a time where someone could walk up to me, look me in the face, say he hated my guts, and then make demands of me. I would turn right around and give that person the shirt off my back if he needed it. This was slowly killing me. I had to do something about it, and I did. I cut those people out of my life. I no longer let myself be used or talked into doing anything just because others try to make me feel guilty.

I also cut ties with all the negative people in my life, those who carry the weight of the world on their shoulders. Life is out to get them. Everybody hates them, and they hate everybody and everything. Forget their glass being half-full or half-empty; it was completely empty in their eyes. They never had anything good to say about anybody or anything. To them life was miserable, and I had to cut them from my life.

I also had a few physical and love relationships that ended due to my cancer. These men were cancers in my life, and they had to be cut out. At first, I didn't want to cut them from my life because I believed that being with someone was better than being alone, and I didn't want to be alone. But then I realized that they cared only for the physical part of my body. They're eyes could not see my soul because they were focusing on my flesh.

Why was it that losing my breasts was harder on men and others than it was on me? It was my body and my life. Once these men took a look at my reconstructed breasts, they couldn't look me in the eye. What were they afraid of? What were they ashamed of? I wasn't ashamed. If I had been ashamed, I wouldn't have shown them in the first place. I wanted to share my life with these men, and instead I felt like covering my body in shame. Never again!

Chapter 16

What Cancer Taught Me

Cancer sucks. There is no other way to say it. It just sucks. However, cancer also taught me a great deal about myself, my friends, my family, and life in general. I stood up to this disease and I fought it, but as you've read, it wasn't easy. It was an uphill battle all the way … or so it seemed.

As I mentioned in the beginning, I didn't write this book to fill your head with medical facts or cancer statistics. I wrote this to help you or someone you love face a difficult battle. During my cancer battle, I went through many things and many changes, both physically and mentally. Since I was first diagnosed in 2001, I've had twenty-four surgeries, four rounds of aggressive chemotherapy, so many scans, X-rays, and MRIs that I could light up the Las Vegas Strip, more tubes of blood than I could even think of counting, a chest wall biopsy, and two extremely painful bone marrow biopsies.

I didn't show it, but I often got depressed and talked to my cancer. One of those times came right after losing my hair to chemotherapy. When I finally worked up the courage to take a look in the mirror the first time after shaving my head, I burst into tears. I wanted to punch the image that appeared before me in the mirror. This person wasn't me. This person had a shaved head, was extremely pale, bloated, had puffy eyes from crying, and was ugly. *Oh, my God, this person is me*, I thought.

I closed the bathroom door and stripped completely naked. I turned around to look in the mirror. It was as if I was looking at a complete stranger. My hair was gone from my head and from my private parts. My body was extremely bloated from the chemotherapy, and my chest was still bruised from the surgery. My incisions were starting to heal and forming into thick, puffy scars. Who was this stranger in the mirror? What had cancer turned me into?

Damn you, cancer. Damn you for doing this to me and turning me into a stranger. A stranger I can't even stand to look at in the mirror. A stranger that is repulsive to look at. A stranger that I sometimes feel is no longer a woman because she has been butchered and cut open. A stranger that I fear no man will ever love again.

Damn you, cancer for trying to take away my faith. Damn you for trying to take away my happiness. Damn you for making me feel worthless. Damn you for taking away my chances for love. Damn you for making me afraid. Damn you for making me hate myself right now. And damn you for making me feel guilty.

I felt guilty for putting my family through this. My daughter had to go through cancer with me at what should have been one of the best and most carefree times of her life. She shouldn't have had to worry about this stuff at age twelve. She should have been having fun with her friends and going to the movies, hanging out and listening to music. Why did she have to suffer too? Not only was she worrying for me, but now I had given her a greater risk of developing breast cancer herself. Now she had to worry about me living and her health in the future.

And my family. We had just lost our dad four months before I was diagnosed with cancer. We should have been healing, but now my sisters and brother were worried about me and whether I would live. My sisters now had a 33 percent greater risk of developing breast cancer because of me. Why did *I* have to bring this devastation on my family? Why did *I* have to be the one to cause them additional worry? Why was cancer doing this to my family?

Cancer was—and still is—never far from my thoughts, but I tried hard not to let it consume my thoughts and my days. I fought hard every day, even though I often didn't want to. The fight was tough, and it felt as if I spent most of those fighting years either in a hospital, operating room, or doctor's office. It was a long battle, but honestly, I wouldn't change it for anything. I wouldn't change it because I learned so much.

Here are just a few of the things I learned:

- Sometimes life isn't fair, but you have to play with the cards you're dealt.
- I'm a stronger person than I thought I was.
- God won't answer all my prayers the way I want him to, because he knows what's best for me.
- No matter what is going on in my life, I need to put my faith in God and turn things over to him.
- My daughter truly does love me.
- I can be replaced on my job, but nobody can replace me as mother to Brittany.
- I look good bald.
- Tattoos hurt.
- Dogs have an uncanny ability to sense when something is wrong.
- How to deal with pain.
- Hawaii is as beautiful in person as it is in pictures.
- To face my fears and that it's okay to be afraid.
- People are brought into your life for a reason, and I would never have met some of my closest friends had I not had cancer.
- That I had cancer, but cancer didn't have me.

I'm grateful for my experience, and I thank God every day he let me live. I'm alive and feel compelled to tell my story in the hopes that it will help someone. If one person reads my story and learns something from it, or it helps him realize that he, too, can beat cancer, then what I went through was 100 percent worth it.

If you are facing cancer, accept it so you can start the fight. Put on your armor, but realize your fight is not going to be easy. You'll want to give up, but don't. Keep fighting.

Draw strength and courage from your friends and family. Join a support group. Don't be afraid to talk to people about what you're going through. Not only will it help you, but it will help others around you. Keep a journal of your thoughts and feelings. Keep a cancer scrapbook of all the cards, letters, and emails you receive. Keep a photo journal of your cancer battle. All these things will help get you through the fight.

One of the most important things I would like to stress is to be your own boss when it comes to your health. Push for tests if you feel something isn't right. Seek second and third opinions if you don't feel comfortable with what you're being told. Always keep copies of your scans, exams, X-rays, and blood tests. Take them with you to every appointment so you don't have to guess about your results. Share them with family in the event they need the information on your behalf or they ever need it for themselves.

When going to appointments, take a friend with you to make sure you get everything the doctor is saying. If that isn't possible, be sure to take a notebook or tape recorder with you. Don't be afraid to ask questions. Write them down any time you think of them so you can ask your doctor at your next visit. Do your own research when a doctor or nurse tells you something you don't completely understand. Be your own health advocate and stand up for yourself. Don't let anyone push you around when it comes to your own health care.

Numerous organizations out there offer support and services to cancer patients and their families. Seek them out and make contact. One such organization is the American Cancer Society, but there are many others. Don't be afraid or embarrassed to ask for help. It doesn't mean you're weak. It takes a strong person to ask for help.

Surround yourself with things that make you happy, and don't be embarrassed to have fun. A friend of mine gave me a little figurine that says, "Dance like nobody is watching." Do that. Dance and have fun. Laugh at yourself.

I don't care if anybody is watching. Life is too short, and I'm not going to live it for someone else. I'm living my life. If I want to dance like I have acid in my shorts, then I'm going to do it. If I want to laugh out loud in the theater, I will. If I want to run and play in the rain, I will. If I want to stay in my pajamas all day and watch sappy movies while eating junk food, I will. However, there is one thing I won't do.

I won't back down from a good fight, especially where cancer is concerned. Cancer didn't know who it was messing with when it picked my body for its temporary home. I started the fight right away, and even though I'm in remission, I won't stop fighting. I have to continue to fight. I have to fight for those of you who are just starting your battle. I have to fight for those who don't have the strength to fight, and I certainly have to fight for those who are no longer alive to fight. We all need to take up this fight.

Cancer is an epidemic. I believe there is not a person alive who could say that he doesn't know of someone who has cancer or has battled cancer. This disease lashes out at young and old, black and white, rich and poor. It just doesn't care about you or your situation. It needs to be stopped, and you can help.

Get involved in your community to help raise awareness about this disease. Volunteer for events such as the American Cancer Society's Relay For Life or Susan G. Komen's Race for the Cure. These events raise money for programs in your community; money that will fund programs to help patients and their families, and money that will help fund researchers and research projects that might lead to a cure for this disease. After all, a cure is what we strive for. It's what we hope for. It's something I hope for every day of my life.

Yes, to live in a world where there is no more cancer, I'd give my left boob for that … oh, wait, I already did.

Cancer is so limited. . .
It cannot cripple Love.
It cannot shatter Hope.
It cannot corrode Faith.
It cannot destroy Peace.
It cannot kill Friendship.
It cannot suppress Memories.
It cannot silence Courage.
It cannot invade the Soul.
It cannot steal eternal Life.
It cannot conquer the Spirit.

—Anonymous